AF564667

MICROTEACHING IN SECONDARY SCHOOL TEACHER EDUCATION

By

Dr. Mushtaq Ahmed I. Patel
Associate Professor
Dept. of Education
DDE, MANUU
Hyderabad (A.P.)

&

Ms. Mohasina Anjum A. Ansari
Research Assistant
CSSEIP, MANUU
Hyderabad (A.P.)
(India)

DISCOVERY PUBLISHING HOUSE PVT. LTD.
NEW DELHI-110 002

Published by:

Tilak Wasan

DISCOVERY PUBLISHING HOUSE PVT. LTD.
4383/4A, Ansari Road, Darya Ganj
New Delhi-110 002 (India)
Phone : +91-11-23279245, 43596064-65
Fax : +91-11-23253475
E-mail : parul.wasan@gmail.com
discoverypublishinghouse@gmail.com
web : www.discoverypublishinggroup.com

***First Edition:* 2012**
ISBN: 978-93-5056-106-5

Microteaching in Secondary School Teacher Education
© 2012, Authors

All rights reserved. No part of this publication should be reproduced, stored in a retrieval system, or transmitted in any form or by any means: electronic, mechanical, photocopying, recording or otherwise, without the prior written permission of the author and the publisher.

This book has been published in good faith that the material provided by authors is original. Every effort is made to ensure accuracy of material, but the publisher and printer will not be held responsible for any inadvertent error(s). In case of any dispute, all legal matters are to be settled under Delhi jurisdiction only.

Printed at:
Shree Balaji Art Press
Delhi

Foreword

The present era is engulfed with technological equipments. Some are of the view that the technology is supreme and omnipresence. Human beings are considered as slaves to these technological devices. In this era too it is fact that teacher's presence in the school is having more impact than the presence of machine alone. Therefore, there is a great importance of teacher in the schools. The presence of teacher in the classroom has to be effective during the teaching–learning process. For increasing this effectiveness teachers are being trained in microteaching along with other methods of teaching.

I am happy to learn that my affectionate students Mushtaq Ahmed I. Patel and Mohasina Anjum A. Ansari are presenting the research work in the field of microteaching in the form of a book. This book will be beneficial to all those who are working for the cause of teacher education. The book covers topics related to education, technology, educational technology. A great deal of emphasis is laid on concept and methods of micro–teaching and its impact on teacher education programme. The authors elaborate upon the strategy adopted by them for research and the analysis of data. Finally they give their findings and suggestions related to microteaching.

I congratulate both the authors for taking up the publication work. I also expect that they will work for some more publi-cations in the field of education.

Dr. R.T. Jantli

M.A., M.Sc., M.Ed., Ph.D. (Edu)m
Professor & Principal (Retd.),
University College of Education,
Karnataka University, Dharwad

Preface

Teachers' role is less acknowledged. Their roles are shadowed by the presence of politicians, bureaucrats and other high profile intellectuals. But, it is the teacher whose efforts have resulted in making of these personalities. They are imparting academic knowledge and inculcating right type of values among their taughts. The role of teacher is more powerful at secondary level. The language, behaviour and mannerism adopted by teacher is imitated by learner. There are a large number of technological equipments, which have crept in for the aid of better education. However, in this context too the role and influence of teachers has not reduced. The technology is also influencing teacher teaching techniques. One such low cost technique that is commonly used is microteaching. This is part of the whole curriculum of teacher education in the nation. Microteaching has certainly helped in learning and improving teaching skills.

The first chapter of this book throws light on various concepts associated with education, which all summarise that education strives to bring the allround development of an individual. The technology in general and educational technology in particular has important role to play in education. The technology has a positive impact on teaching-learning process. Similarly, microteaching process is also having a positive impact on teacher training. Microteaching is a training technique which is a result of the development and application of educational technology. Various skills of teaching are briefed in this chapter. The second chapter in this book lays emphasis on studies pertaining to Microteaching. In this chapter different studies related to the problem of study are presented from Indian and foreign perspectives. The third chapter is meant for presenting the methodology adopted for the particular study. The authors have presented their plan, experience, practical difficulties and strategies adopted during the course of study. The data obtained during the study are analysed in the fourth chapter. The major hypotheses is viewed and all the 32 minor hypothesis are examined from the available data. The final chapter concludes by giving a summary of the work done. The authors also list the trends of research in microteaching techniques. Lastly, it is concluded that there is significant effect of microteaching on the training of student teachers.

We are grateful to all those who have encouraged in pursuing this study. The authors are grateful to all the officials and colleagues of the MANUU for their encouragement and support. We are specially thankful to the Vice Chancellor, MANUU, Prof. Mohammad Miyan for his encouragement and support. Prof. R. T. Jantli, who is the research guide requires special mention for encouragement and guidance. The teacher educators and teacher education institutes have co-operated and supported in this study and we are grateful to them. Our beloved son Areeb Hussain deserves praise for his calm and co-operation during the study and daughter Nabeeha Fatima for bearing all sorts of pressures. We are thankful to our parents for their encouragement. Last but not least, we are thankful to all those who have directly or indirectly helped in successful completion of this work.

We hope that this book will disseminate and circulate few important aspects of educational technology and more so about microteaching. The readers may give their observations and suggestions regarding improvement of contents of the book.

Mushtaq Ahmed I. Patel
Mohasina Anjum A. Ansari

Content

Contents

Microteaching Technique for Better Teacher Training

Introduction

Education brings about the latent qualities within the human being. This has been emphasised from time immemorial. With the improvement in the society the technology has also improved. All the modern day facilities and amenities are the result of technological advancements and growth of science. The availability of revolving chair at the head-master's chamber, the call bell, telephone, mobile, computers, its software and hardwares are the products of technology which are being used in the field of education. It helps in systematising teaching-learning process in schools and increases quality. There is a widespread use of educational technologies in India. The teacher education has taken advantage of these technologies for improving the teacher behaviour. Microteaching has played crucial role in development of all these aspects. The content of this unit tries to know usage of technology in education especially with respect to pre-service teacher education. The microteaching is a training technique used to improve the teachers' teaching skills. The discussions are made about various skills used in training through microteaching

EDUCATION

The educator has to be aware of the limitations and scope of education. Teacher as an educator, has to know various connotations used in the field of education. An attempt has been made to describe education from the perspectives of various educationists.

In the words of John Dewey: "Education is the development of all those capacities in the individual which will enable him to control his environment and fulfil his responsibilities."

Education is the most important invention of mankind. It is more important than his invention of tools, machines, space crafts medicine, weapons and even of language because language too was the product of his education. Man without education would still be living just like an animal. It is education, which transformed man from a mere "two-legged animal" into human.

Education of man does not begin at school, it begins at birth. It ends not when he graduates from the university but at his death. Hence, education is a life-long process.

Indian Concept of Education

Indian philosophy is primarily dominated by metaphysical interest. The system of education in India has conformed to the ideals and objectives that the people have set before them. These ideals and objectives have changed from time to time to fit the new era in which people are influenced by the *Vedas*, the *Upanishads*, the *Gita*, and the *Puranas* and also by the orthodox and unorthodox schools of philosophy. In India the concept of education has always been different from the western concept of education due to the difference in social values, prevailing norms of the society and the concept of personality.

Indian approach inclines towards the spiritual aspect as a part of the development by education.

In the words of A. S. Altekar, "Education has always been regarded in India as a source of illumination and power which transforms and enables our nature by the progressive and harmonious development of our physical, mental, intellectual and spiritual powers and faculties."

Indian Definition of Education

- "Education is something which makes man self reliant and self-less".

  —*Rigveda*
- "Education is for liberation."

  —*Upanishad*
- "Education is the realisation of self."

  —*Shankaracharya*
- "The widest road leading to the solution of all our problems is education."

  —*Tagor*
- "By education, I mean allround drawing out of the best in the child and man, body, mind and spirit."

  —*Gandhi*
- "Education means the manifestation of divine perfection, already existing in man."

  —*Vivekananda*

Western Concept of Education

According to the western concept of education, it is deliberate and organised activity through which the physical, intellectual, aesthetic, moral and spiritual potentialities of the child are developed, both in the individual as an individual and also as a member of society so that he may lead the fullest and richest life possible in this world and finally attain his ultimate end in the world to come.

The meaning of education was initially available in the words of Plato and with little modification of the Plato's definition still the western concept is same.

Western Definitions of Education

- "Education means the bringing out of the ideas of universal validity which are latent in the mind of every man."

  —*Socrates*

- "Education is the capacity to feel pleasure and pain at the right moment. It develops in the body and in the soul of the student all the beauty and all the perfection which he is capable of."

—Plato

- "Education is the creation of a sound mind in a sound body. It develops man's faculty, especially his mind, so that he may be able to enjoy the contemplation of supreme truth, goodness and beauty of which perfect happiness essentially consists."

—Aristotle

- "Education is complete living."

—Herber Spencer

- "Education is a process of which and by which knowledge, character and behaviour of the young are shaped and moulded".

—Prof. Drever

- "The influence of the environment on the individual with a view to producing a permanent change in his habits of behaviour of thought and attitude.

—G. H. Thompson

Some Latest Definitions of Education

(i) "The central task of education is to implant a will and facility for learning; it should produce not learned but learning people. The truly human society is a learning society, where grand parents, parents and children are students together".

—Eric Hoffer

(ii) "The only purpose of education is to teach a student how to live his life by developing his mind and equipping him to deal with reality. The training he needs is theoretical, i.e. conceptual. He has to be taught to think, to under-stand, to integrate, to prove. He has to be taught the essentials of the knowledge discovered in the past and he has to be equipped to acquire further knowledge by his own effort."

—Ayn. R

(iii) "The aim of education should be to teach rather how to think, than what to think–rather to improve our minds, so as to enable us to think for ourselves, than to load the memory with the thoughts of other men".

—*Bill Beattie*

TECHNOLOGY

The word technology is derived from Greek word 'technic' meaning art or skill and 'logia' meaning science or study. Thus, technology is the science of study of an art or skills.

Hierra, A. (1973)—"Technology is the set of instruments and skills which are used to satisfy the needs of the community".

Sachs, I. (1973)—"Technology is knowledge organised for production".

Page, T. (1976)—"Technology is application of scientific knowledge to practical purpose.

Romizowski, J. Alexander (1980)—"Technology describes a 'process'—something that people do to solve problems or to achieve aims and 'products' such as instruments and tools, something tangible that exists and can be used to satisfy the needs of the community."

EDUCATIONAL TECHNOLOGY

The world of education has also been influenced by the increased use of technology. It has provided valuable help in improving the task of the teacher, smoothening the process of teaching-learning and enriching the goals of education.

Eric Ashby has identified four revolutions in education. They are:

(i) The first revolution occurred when societies began to differentiate adult roles and there was shift in roles in the process of education from parents to teachers and from home to school.

(ii) The second was the adoption of the "written word" as a tool of education. Prior to that, only oral instruction

prevailed and with great reluctance writing was permitted to co-exist with the spoken word in the classroom.

(iii) The third revolution came with the invention of primary and the subsequent widespread availability of books.

(vi) The fourth revolution in the field of education was brought about by the development in electronics, notably those involving radio, television, tape-recorder, computer etc. To the electronic world of education, the behavioural scientists also added their concept of teaching-learning process creating the new world of Educational Technology.

Meaning

Educational Technology is a system of 5 Ms i.e a system in education in which machines, materials, media, men and methods are interrelated and work together for the fulfilment of specific educational objectives. An adequate knowledge of theory and practices of educational technology and their proper use would enable the teacher to understand and effectively discharge his new roles in the educational system in an age of 'information explosion', 'knowledge explosion', 'population explosion', and 'expectation explosion'.

Nature and Characteristic of Educational Technology

Educational Technology is the application of scientific principles to education. It lays stress on the development of methods and techniques for effective teaching-learning. It stresses the organisation of learning situations for the effective realisation of the goals of education. It emphasises the designing and measuring instruments for testing learning outcomes. It facilitates learning by controlling environment media and methods. It involves input, output and process of education.

Definitions of Educational Technology

- B. C. Mathis—"Educational Technology refers to the development of a set of systematic methods, practical knowledge for designing, operating and testing in schools."

- Dieuziede, Director General of UNESCO's Division of Methods, Materials and Techniques—"Educational Technology implies all the intellectual and operational efforts made during recent years to re-group, re-arrange and systematise the application of scientific methods and the control of environment in so far as this reflects on learning".
- I. K Davis—"Educational Technology is concerned with the problems of education and training and is characterised by a discipline and systematic approach to the organisation of resources for learning".
- G.O.M. Leith—"Educational Technology is application of scientific knowledge about learning and the conditions of learning to improve the effectiveness and efficiency of teaching and learning".
- J. B. Gases—"Educational Technology has to be seen as part of a persistent and complex endeavour of bringing pupils, teachers and technical means together in an effective way".
- National Council of Educational Technology UK—"Educational Technology is development, application and evaluation of systems, techniques and aids to improve the process of human learning".
- J. Bloomer—"Educational Technology is the application of scientific knowledge about learning to practical learning situations".
- Shive, K. Mitra—"Educational Technology can be conceived as a science of techniques and methods by which educational goals could be realised".
- S.K. Mangal—"Educational Technology should stand for a wise application of the available human and non-human resources for providing appropriate solution to the educational problems and to improve the process and products of education".

- NCERT—"Educational Technology is the means of development, application and evaluation of three different things: *(i)* techniques, *(ii)* system, and *(iii)* aids to improve the process of human learning".
- Collier very clearly describes what Educational Technology is. He says Educational Technology is not about audiovisual aids. Educational Technology he says is not electronic gadgeting or television. Educational Technology he opines is as wide as education itself, it is concerned with the design and evaluation of curriculum and learning experiences and with the problem of implementing and renovating them. He concludes that it is essentially a rational problem-solving approach to education, a way of thinking sequentially and systematically about teaching and learning.

Use of Educational Technology in India

In India before the sixties, the term educational technology was almost unknown to teaching aids. In the early sixties, the use of the term Educational Technology took its roots through programmed learning. Gradually the meaning and concept of educational technology has grown wider and larger.

Educational technology as we find today has a meaningful present and promising future in our country. Some significant developments:

- There has been wider and more effective utilization of radio for broadcasting educational programme throughout the country.
- Educational Technology is concerned with the problem of the training and re-training of the large number of school teachers effectively and economically.
- Educational Technology in Distance Education.
- Another major area where educational technology is being used in our country relates with language instructions.
- Correspondence education.

- Educational Technology concerned with the preparation, development and utilisation of audio-visual material and handling as well as maintenance of the hardware appliances and sophisticated gadgets.

In his latest trend, educational technology is proving its worth by utilising the services of computer technology in the field of education.

TEACHING

Teaching is a highly skilled job and therefore requires adequate training. Every teacher must have a clear understanding of his task, its meaning and intricacies involved. It is a system of actions intended to induce learning.

N.L. Gage defines teaching as an inter-personal influence aimed at changing the behaviour potential of another person, i.e. not only the teacher influences the student, also the reverse happens. Thus, teaching is a bipolar process, of its one pole is teacher and another is student.

Teaching is dynamic and well planned process with the main objectives of providing a variety of learning experiences. In its narrower meaning teaching means to impart knowledge.

Modern teaching is not a mechanical process. It is exacting and intricate as well. Teaching is not 'telling and testing'. Teaching is the complex art of guiding students through a variety of selected experiences towards the attainment of appropriate teaching-learning goals.

John Dewey (1859-1952) states "the more a teacher aware of the past experiences of students of their hopes, desires, chief interests, the better will he understood the forces at work that need to be directed and utilised for the formation of reflective habits".

Albert Eienstein (1879-1955) has observed: "It is the supreme art of the teacher to awaken joy in creative expression and knowledge".

Swami Vivekananda (1863-1902) describes the role of the teacher in teaching as, "The true teacher is he who can immediately comedown to the level of the student".

The modern teaching technology is based on modern scientific principles and discoveries. It emphasises the development of critical thinking power of the learner. Innovations like team teaching, micro-teaching and simulated teaching is used.

The task of preparing teachers who can impart the necessary competencies to the students under their stewardship refers to the area of Teacher Education. It is considered to be the weaker link in educational system. Recently, the National Commission on Teacher and Central Ministry of Education in its document 'Challenge of Education—A policy perspective' have pointed out these deficiencies and laid stress on revitalisation and modernisation of teacher education programmes.

Teaching is a very crucial job for which one must be fully trained. One must be skilful during teaching because teaching is an art. Earlier the theme was "teachers are born not made". But, the process of training in existing institutions is very poor. The stress should be given on the skills of the teaching and skills of communication. The state of teacher education programme has been criticised by many research workers and scholars working in the area of education. According to Pophan and Baker (1968), "trained and untrained teachers did not differ significantly regarding bringing about learning in pupils". The major weakness in teacher education programmes according Borg (1970) in the present are because;

- Emphasis is on teaching rather than on doing.
- Instructions are general rather than specific.
- Effective models are not provided.
- Effective feedback is not provided.

Teacher Behaviour

The term teacher behaviour in this way may be defined as the behaviour or activities of persons as they go about doing whatever is required of teachers, particularly those activities which are concerned with the guidance or direction of the learning of others (Ryans, 1969).

According to McNergency and Carner—Teacher Behaviour may be regarded as a function of the characteristics of the teacher, his environment and the task in which the teacher energy.

Contemporary Situation of Teacher Education

The goals of education with the aim of taking the nation into 21st Century cannot be achieved unless teachers have the necessary skills and competencies. The skills and competencies can be developed through systematic approach to revitalise and modernise teacher education.

The revitalisation and modernisation of teacher education programmes involve not only curriculum reforms but also translate into performance through appropriate transactions.

In recent years several innovations have been developed to equip teachers with requisite competencies and skills to teach effectively. The innovative training techniques like simulated teaching and microteaching is very much suitable to the Indian situations.

Teaching practice of student teachers is an important aspect of the classroom teaching of college of education. But, in the same the student teachers are weak. The traditional pattern of such student teaching programme has resulted in producing incompetent and ineffective classroom teachers. The situation like this had caused to think about some alternative measures and techniques to bring improvement in the student teaching programme. Microteaching is one of such innovations and technique that has emerged on the map of teacher education for improving the student teaching programme.

MICROTEACHING

Historical Perspective in Microteaching

It may be recalled that in 1961, at Standford University, a doctoral candidate Keith Acheson, discovered a newspaper article about a German scientist who had invented a portable videotape recorder, then called the Mactronic. Acheson was working with Dr. Robert N. Bush and Dwight W. Allen, who had received a grant from the Ford Foundation to examine those experiences which might be relevant for teaching interns in an innovative teacher education programme.

As a part of the teacher education curriculum, each intern was expected to participate in reduced teaching exercises called "Demonstration Teaching". Each student taught five or six students a brief lesson while the remaining students played various roles. One by one interns would play 'Johney Good Guy', 'Joe Bee-Bop', 'Helen happy girls' and 'Carol know-it all' interrupting every other student by trying to answer a question even when she knew she was wrong. Most of the professors and certainly the interns agreed that the experience was an over-dramatised and anxiety producing session that helped no one what had been rewarding experience for the interns often turned out to be a verbal battle between them and the supervisor.

The intern versus supervisor conflict revolved around the problem of convincing the intern that certain undesirable activities actually took place in such demonstration sessions. Either the intern did not see what was occurring or he did not wish to recognise it.

Acheson (1964) saw the possibility of using the videotape to provide immediate feedback to the intern on what occurred in the demonstration lesson and the supervisor, with support from Bush and Allen.

A number of experiments have been conducted in many institutions in the USA, UK and the Netherlands. In India also a number of institutions have started work in the area of microteaching in recent years. The level Halme Trust gave a five year grant to Sterling University in UK for doing work on microteaching. A comprehensive bibliography on micro-teaching has been prepared by W. Raymond McAleese of the University of Aberdeen and Derick Unwin of the University of Ulster.

In a recent survey in the United States on the use of microteaching in teacher education programmes, it was found that 141 of the 442 National Council of Teacher Education accredited colleges and universities were using microteaching in the secondary education programmes.

Microteaching in India

A number of educational institutions have started work in the area of Microteaching. D. D. Tiwari was the first to take up this work in 1967 at the Government Central Pedagogical Institute at Allahabad. This was followed by G. B. Shah who tried an experiment in microteaching with the help of a tape recorder in the Faculty of Education and Psychology, Baroda in 1970. A major contribution to the microteaching as a teaching device was made in 1974 at the Technical Teachers' Training Institute, Chandigarh under the guidance of Dr. N. L. Dosajh. The Technical Teachers' Training Institute, Calcutta has started microteaching with the help of audio tape.

The first book on microteaching in India was written by N. L. Dosajh under the caption *'Modification of Teacher Behaviour Through Microteaching* (1977).

Developmental History

The chronological development of microteaching is as under:

1963 – A. W. Dwight Allen, Standford University was first to coin the term Microteaching.

1967 – D. D. Tiwari, Government Central Pedagogical Institute, Allahabad worked in India in the area of Microteaching.

1970 – W. Raymond McAllesse, University of Aberdeen and Derick Unwin, New University of Ulster, prepared comprehensive bibliography on Microteaching.

– Perlberg Ayre and Davi C. Oberiant, Department of General Engineering, University of Illionois utilised microteaching techniques to improve engineering instruction.

– University of Sterling utilised this technique for training secondary school teachers.

1971 – E. C. Wrag, Exeter University has done a good deal of work in this area.

– R. R. Chaudasma tried out microteaching but again without a closed circuit television.

1973 – L. P. Singh tried microteaching and provided feedback through Flander's Interaction Analysis technique.

– N. S. Marker and N. Pangotra started work in the field of microteaching but again without the Closed Circuit Television (CCTV).

1974 – The Technical Training Institute, Madras set up studio for educational television programme in which microteaching was introduced for the training of technical teachers.

– N. L. Dosajh, The Technical Teacher Training Institute, Chandigarh introduced microteaching as a training device for student teaching for their training. A closed circuit television equipment was provided by the Royal Nether Government.

Meaning of Microteaching

Microteaching is a scaled-down, simulated teaching encounter designed for the training of both pre-service or in-service teachers. Its purpose is to provide teachers with the opportunity for the safe practice of an enlarged cluster of teaching skills while learning how to develop simple, single-concept lessons in any teaching subject. Microteaching helps teachers improve both content and methods of teaching and develop specific teaching skills such as questioning, the use of examples and simple artefacts to make lessons more interesting, effective reinforcement techniques, and introducing and closing lessons effectively. Immediate, focused feedback and encouragement, combined with the opportunity to practice the suggested improvements in the same training session, are the foundations of microteaching protocols.

Microteaching is an organised practice teaching. The goal is to give instructors confidence, support and feedback by letting them tryout among friends and colleagues a short slice of what they plan to do with their students. Ideally, microteaching sessions take place before the first day of class, and are videotaped for review individually with an experienced teaching consultant. Microteaching is a quick, efficient, proven and fun way to help teachers got off to a strong start.

A microteaching is an opportunity to present a sample "snapshot" of what/how you teach and to get some feedback from colleagues about how it was received. It is a chance to try teaching strategies that you may not use regularly.

This is a good, safe time to experiment with something new to you to get feedback on a technique you have been trying but are not sure about its effectiveness.

The dictionary meaning of microteaching is teacher training using videotape, that is a training exercise, used in teacher training in which a student or student teacher is videotaped during part of a class for subsequent analysis and evaluation.

A microteaching is an 8-10 minutes lesson in which you will put into practice the elements of effective teaching. At registration you will be assigned to a small group of eight to ten other student-teachers. You will work with this group during portions of the Orientation and will do your microteaching with them. Each group will be led by a faculty member of peer. You will present your lessons with your group members serving as students. The presentations will be videotaped. You will then view and critique your own videotape using the principles learned in the Orientation. Your private replay and self-analysis will be followed by a one-on-one conference with your group leader. The conference will help you identify strengths in your presentation and provide suggestions for the areas you would like to improve.

Microteaching is a training technique which is called 'micro' since a teacher trainee practices with a small group of 5 to 10 pupils for a short duration of 5 to 20 minutes on a selected concept of a lesson and concentrates on a single skills which is magnified.

Teaching skills for student teachers focus on participant observation skills, model teaching discipline techniques and content teaching. Microteaching is not a substitute but a supplement to the teacher education programme.

Microteaching is a training technique which requires student teachers to teach a single concept using specified teaching skill to a small number of pupils in a short duration of time. The most important point in microteaching is that teaching is practised in terms of definable, observable, measurable and controllable teaching skills.

Basically microteaching is a "scaled down teaching encounter in which a student teacher teaches a small unit to a group of five to 10 students for five to ten minutes or we can say microteaching is a training procedure aimed at simplifying the complexities of the regular teaching process. In a microteaching procedure the trainee is engaged in a scaled-down teaching situation. It is scaled-down in duration of class time and is reduced to five-ten minutes. It is also scaled down in terms of teaching tasks. These tasks may include: the practising and mastering of a specific teaching skill such as lecturing, questioning or leading a discussion.

Microteaching helps in producing skilled teachers. Microteaching has the potential to produce more thoughtful, critical and skilled teacher (Comford, 1990). By using educational theories we can make use of microteaching in teacher education that is for each microteaching performance by integrating current theories of teaching into the analytic framework that underscores the goals and the cognitive understones of the microteaching performance (Karthigeyan, 2006). The success of microteaching is depends on the feedback step due to which the practising skill get improved and further developed. The subsequent feedback becomes a dialogue between student, peers, teacher fellows and tutors that provides different refractions of this practice and contribute to the development of pre-critical, internalised and hypothetical thresholds (John, Susan, Gary, 2003). The video tape recording as a source of feedback in microteaching plays a significant role in knowing the strengths and weakness in the performed skill. Videotape recording was an effective method of feedback in microteaching and student teachers will show more significant progress in the master of teaching skills (Edward, 2001). Microteaching is a vehicle for development and training in Teacher Education (Andrew, 1987).

Definitions of Microteaching

- Allen, D.W. (1966): Microteaching is a scaled down teaching encounter in class size and class time.
- Allen, D.W. and Eve, A. W. (1968): Microteaching is defined as a system of controlled practice that makes it possible to concentrate on specified teaching behaviour and to practice teaching under controlled conditions.
- Munn (1966): Microteaching as a "scaled down teaching encounter in class size and class time".
- Buch, R. N. (1968): Microteaching is a trainer education technique which allows the teacher to apply well defined teaching skills to a carefully prepared lesson in a planned series of five to ten minutes, encounter with a small group of real classroom students often with an opportunity to observe the performance on videotape.
- Mc. Aluse and Mrwin (1970): Microteaching is most often applied to the use of closed circuit television to give immediate feedback to a teacher trainer performance in simplified environment".
- Sadker and Cooper (1972): Microteaching is a teaching situation scaled down in terms of both time and number of students which has usually meant a five to twenty minute lesson involving three to ten students.

- Cliff, J. C. (1976): Microteaching is a teachers training programme which reduces the teaching solution to simpler and more controlled encounter achieved by limiting the practice teaching to specific skill and reducing time and class size.
- LA Due (1970): Microteaching is an opportunity to gain classroom capabilities and expertise before the student teacher start entering the teaching situation.
- Mc. Aleese and Unvin (1971): Microteaching is a scaled down teaching encounter in terms of time, class, size, lesson, length and teaching complexities.
- Mc Knight (1971): Microteaching is a scaled down teaching encounter designed to develop new skills and refine old ones.
- Encyclopaedia of Education (Ed. Deighton, L.C.-1971): Microteaching is a real, constructed, scaled down teaching encounter, which is used for teacher training, curriculum development and research.
- Flanders, Ned A. (1970): Microteaching programme is organised to expose the trainees to an organised curriculum of miniature teaching encounters, moving from the less complex to the more complex.
- Jangira, N. K. and Singh, Ajith (1982): Microteaching is a scaled down teaching encounter or miniature classroom teaching.
- MiLtza (1978): Microteaching is an opportunity to present some thing and then analyse the outcome; the two crucial elements are the ability to see oneself in action and analyse what was done.
- Jangira (1980): Microteaching is a training setting for the student teachers where complexities of normal classroom teaching is reduced by practicing a particular teaching skill, for five to ten minutes on five to ten pupils using single concept.

- Kumar, (1996): Microteaching is a technique of training in which one learns the skills of teaching through a scaled down process at teaching learning.
- Singh (1979): Microteaching is a design for teacher training which provides trainees with information about their performance immediately after completion of their class.
- B. K. Passi and M. S. Lalita (1976): "Microteaching is a training technique which requires student teacher to teach a single concept using specified teaching skill to a small number of pupils in a short duration of time".

New Simplified Microteaching

In the late 1980s and 1990s microteaching was reinvestigated with a completely new format developed in southern Africa and later in China. Because of lack of available technology in developing countries, Microteaching's format had to be made lest technology dependent in order to be useful. Early modifications were made in Malawi, but it was in Namibia and China where microteaching was completely transformed. Twenty-first century microteaching increases training effectiveness using an even more scaled-down teaching simulation environment. In China it became part of a national effort to modernize teaching practice. In India also microteaching has become must for all student teacher. Before, going to practice teaching, a student teacher has to practice a minimum of five to six microteaching skills. If the institutions do not have technical equipments for feedback, then teacher educators and peers group give their feedback.

Microteaching has been developed as a course in many teacher-training institutions around the world. It readily combines theory with practice. When one considers that teacher trainees in many training programmes do their practice teaching under inadequate supervision with no student feedback, the relative merits and economy of microteaching become more and more apparent.

Nature and Characteristics of Microteaching

- Microteaching is relatively new experience or innovation in the field of teacher education, more specifically in student teachers.
- It is a training technique not a teaching technique. In other words it is a technique or design that is used for the training of teachers (or make them learn the art of teaching).
- It is micro or miniaturised teaching in the sense that it scales down the complexities of real teaching with the provisions like those given below:
  - *(i)* Practising one skill at a time.
  - *(ii)* Reducing the class size to 5-10 minutes.
  - *(iii)* Reducing duration of the lesson to 5-10 minutes.
  - *(iv)* Limiting the content to a single concept.
- There is provision of adequate feedback in Microteaching, as it provides the trainees due information about their performances immediately after completion of their lesson.
- Teaching is said to be composed of very specific skills. These skills can not be mastered through the traditional approach to teacher training. Microteaching provides opportunity to select one skill at a time and practise it through its scaled down encounter and then take others in a similar way.
- Microteaching is a highly individualised training device permitting the imposition of a high degree of control in practising a particular skill.

Objectives of Microteaching

The objectives of microteaching are as under:

➢ To give practical teaching exposure to the teachers under-training by lessening the complexities of classroom situations.

- To identify the drawbacks of the teachers and to give immediate feedback for modifying their behaviour.
- To develop experimental teacher education programmes and encourse research identifying new teaching skills.
- To improve teaching through more control of instructional process and supervision.

Objectives of Introduction of Microteaching in Colleges of Education

Duggal and Sharma (1973) have listed the following objectives of introducing microteaching in Colleges of Education:

- To initiate the teacher trainees to analyse and develop teacher behaviour under laboratory conditions.
- To send teachers gradually in the real classroom after gaining enough confidence.
- To impart intensive training in the component skills of teaching.
- To involve the academic potential of teacher trainees for providing feedback.
- To lessen the workload of teacher educators with the involvement of peer supervisors.
- To lessen the burden upon practising schools while having practice of teaching skills under simulations conditions in College of Education.
- To explore the human resources to maximum and making economy with regard to time, money and materials.

Principles Underlying Microteaching Technique

According to recent developments, teaching should now be looked upon as ã set of skills, used by the teacher in the classroom. A skill is a set of behaviours. Like any other behaviour teaching can also be modified. This requires a systematic analysis of what teaching is and what behaviour of teacher contribute to effective learning in pupils.

The technique of microteaching seems to be based on Skinner's famous theory of Operant Conditioning. According to the terminology of Skinner, "if an operant response occurs and is followed by reinforcement, the probability of its recurring increases. The tendency of the operant response to recur decreases with no-reinforcement.... And it thus becomes extinct" (Bastely, 1970). This is the fundamental principle for feedback session in Microteaching. And for "teach, feedback—reteach pattern of microteaching techniques, Skinner theory of 'shaping' or 'successives approximations' in the acquisition of new pattern of behaviours seem to have been applied.

Microteaching is based on a few sound principles which are briefly explained below:

Principle of One Skill at a Time

In microteaching training of one skill is given to the person who has acquired mastery over it. Then, the second skill is taken up and so on. Then, we find that microteaching is based on the principle of giving training of one skill at a time.

Principle of Limited Contents

In microteaching limited contents are taken up and the teacher is required to use those contents only. It helps the beginner, teacher teach that limited material easily and confidently.

Principle of Practice

Microteaching is based on the sound principle of practice. Here, a lot of practices are given by taking up one skill at a time. Practice makes a man perfect. It helps the pupil teacher in becoming better and better.

Principle of Immediate Feedback

The micro lesson lasts for four or five minutes only. Thereafter, feedback is provided to the pupil teacher. It helps the pupil teacher to know his drawbacks and improve them effectively without any delay.

Principle of Experimentation

A lot of experimentation are involved in Microteaching. The experiment consists of objective observation of actions performed under controlled conditions. The pupil teacher and the supervisor conduct experiment on teaching skills under controlled conditions. Variables like time duration of the lesson, contents of the lessons to be taught number of students sitting in the class etc. can be easily controlled.

Principle of Evaluation

In microteaching, there is continuous assessment of the performance of the pupil teacher. Evaluation helps the learner know his drawbacks and then he is able to improve it. In microteaching each micro lesson is supervised by the supervisor and the peers. Drawbacks in teaching are pointed out and suggestions for improvement given. Self-evaluation is also possible. Thus, evaluation ensures good learning by the pupil teacher.

Principle of Individualised Training

In microteaching each trainee is given training very thoroughly. There is individual attention by the supervisor. The drawbacks in teaching are pointed out, suggestions given one by one and thus improvement is brought about.

Principle of Continuity

Learning of different skills of teaching is a continuous process in microteaching programme. The pupil teacher is learning one skill at one time and "learning continues till he has mastered the skill. For each skill the principle of continuity is implied. It makes the teacher good and effective.

Phases of Microteaching

N. K. Jangira and Ajith Singh presented the three phases as follows:

(i) Knowledge acquisition phase

(ii) Skill acquisition phase

(iii) Transfer phase

1. *Knowledge Acquisition Phase*

In this phase, the student teacher attempts to acquire knowledge about the skill, its role in classroom and its component behaviour. He reads relevant literature. He also observes the demonstration lesson and the mode of presentation of the skill.

Component is modelling.

Activities are: reading, observation and analysing.

2. *Skill Acquisition Phase*

In this phase the student teacher prepares micro lesson, practices the skill and carries out the microteaching cycle.

(i) Feedback

Activities: Teaching, re-teaching

(ii) Microteaching setting

Activities: It includes size and duration of the micro-class, supervisor, types of students etc. in teaching, reteaching.

3. *Transfer Phase*

In this phase the student teacher intergrades the different skills. He teaches in the real classroom instead of an artificial classroom situation.

Component is integration.

Activity is: real teaching.

Steps of Microteaching

Orientation

In the beginning the student teacher should be given necessary theoretical background about microteaching by having a free and fair discussion of aspects like those given below:

- Concept of microteaching.
- Significance or rationale of using microteaching.

- Procedure of microteaching.
- Requirements and setting for adopting microteaching technique.

Discussion of Teaching Skills

Under this step the knowledge and understanding about the following aspects is to be developed.

- Analysis of teaching into component teaching skills.
- The discussion of the rationale and role of the teaching skills in teaching.
- Discussion about the component teaching behaviour comprising various teaching skills.

Selection of a Particular Teaching Skill

The teaching skills are to be practiced by taking them one at a time. Therefore, the student teachers are persuaded to select a particular skill for practice. They are also provided with necessary orientation and processing material for the practice of the skill. Much of such material may be found in the literature available with NCERT. The student teacher may be given a necessary background for the observation of a model or demonstration lesson on the selected particular teaching skill.

Presentation of a Model Demonstration Lesson

Here a demonstration or model lesson for the use of the selected teaching skill is presented before the trainees. This is also termed as 'modelling', i.e. demonstration of the desired behaviours in relation to a skill for imitation by the observer. Depending upon the availability of the resources and type of skill involved, demonstration or model lesson can be given in a number of ways like those given below:

- By providing written material such as handbook, guides, illustrations, video tape.
- By exhibiting a film or a video tape.
- By making the trainees listen an audiotape.

- By arranging a demonstration from a live model, i.e. a teacher educator or an expert demonstrating the use of the skill.

Observation of the Model Lesson and Criticism

What is read, viewed, listened and observed through modelling source is carefully analysed by the trainees. In a demonstration given by an expert or teacher educator student teachers are expected to note down their observations. An observation schedule especially designed for the observation of the specific skill is distributed among the trainees and they are also trained in its use before hand. Such observation of the model lesson and its relevant criticism provides desirable feedback to the person giving the model lesson.

Preparation of Microteaching Lesson Plan

Under this step, student-teachers are required to prepare micro-lesson plans by selecting proper concept for the practice of demonstrated skill. For preparing these lessons, help may be taken from the teacher educators and sample lessons available in the NCERT. The standard setting for a micro-class is as below:

(i) Number of pupils: 5-10.

(ii) Types of pupils: Real pupils or preferable peers.

(iii) Type of supervisor: Teacher educators and peers.

(iv) Time duration of a micro-lesson: 36 minutes.

This duration is divided as under:

Teaching session	6 mts
Feedback session	6 mts
Re-plan session	12 mts
Re-teach session	6 mts
Re-feedback session	6 mts
	36 mts

Practice of the Skill (Teach-Session)

Under this step, the student-teacher teaches his prepared micro lesson for 6 minutes in a micro class consisting of 5-10 real pupils or peers. It is supervised by the teacher educator and peers both with the help of appropriate observation schedule. Where possible the student-teacher may also have his lesson taped on a video or audio tape.

Providing Feedback

The greatest advantage of microteaching lies in providing immediate feedback to the student-teacher on his teaching performance demonstrated in his micro-lesson. The feedback is provided in terms of his use of the component teaching behaviours emphasizing the skill under practice so that he may be properly provided feedback by the peers and teacher educator observing the micro-lesson, videotape, closed circuit television, etc.

Re-planning

In view of the feedback received from the different sources, the student teacher tries to re-plan his micro lesson. He is provided 12 minutes time for this purpose.

Re-teaching

In this session of 6 minutes, the student-teacher re-teaches his micro-lesson on the basis of the represented plan and rearranged setting.

Providing Re-feedback

On the basis of his performance in the re-taught micro-lesson, the student teacher is provided Re-feedback in the way outlined earlier.

Repetition of the Microteaching Cycle

A microteaching cycle used to practise a teaching skill consists of planning, teaching, feedback, re-planning, re-teaching and re-feedback operations see fig. 1.1. Student teacher is required to re-plan and re-teach his lesson till he attains mastery over the skill under practice.

Integration of Teaching Skills

This last step is concerned with task of integrating various teaching skills individually mastered by a student-teacher.

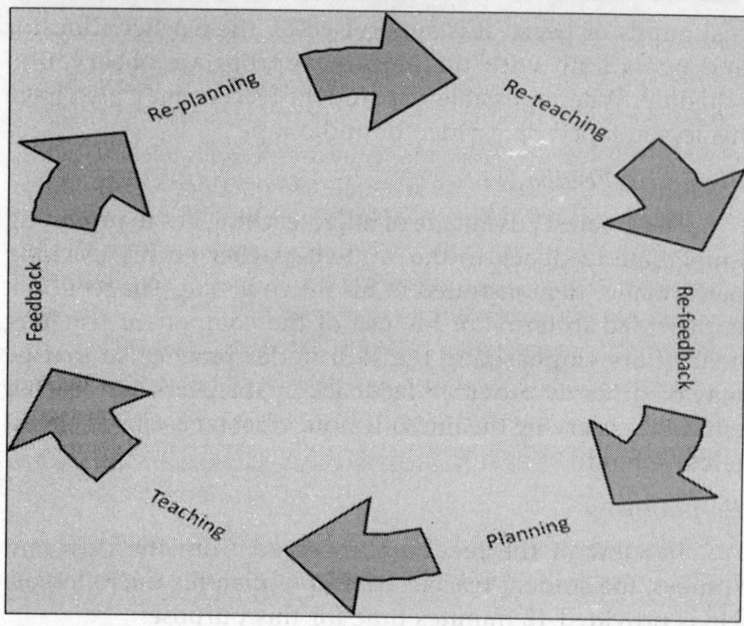

This helps in bridging a gap between training in isolated teaching skills and the real teaching situation faced by a student-teacher.

Figure 1.1: Steps of Microteaching Cycle.

Teaching Skills

Teaching is a complex phenomenon that comprises of various specific teaching skills. Through microteaching complexities of classroom teaching are reduced. The different skills are identified and then mastery of each skill is acquired. Here, two important questions crop up which need consideration. The first one is to know what is a skill? The second one is how many skills are involved in the teaching process.

What is Teaching Skill?

N. L. Gage (1968) says, "Teaching skills are specific instructional activities and procedures that a teacher may use in his classroom. These are related to the various stages of teaching or in the continuous flow of the teacher performance."

How Many Skills?

To know how many skills are involved in the teaching process is rather an interesting study. A few research workers have tried to identify several sets of component teaching skills. Some of them are common with a little different terminology.

Hen and Ryan (1969) of Standford University put forth the view that fourteen skills are involved. Borg and his associates (1970) increased the number to eighteen.

In India, B. K. Passi (1976) on the basis of work done in CASE Baroda has given a list of twenty-one skills. His associates (1979) gave a list of twenty.

None of the list suggested by researchers over exhaustive and final.

We can add or subtract from the lists as per need of the situation. The list of skills given by Allcllalld Ryall (1969) is as under:

- Stimulus variation
- Set induction
- Closure
- Silence and non-verbal cues
- Reinforcement or student participation
- Fluency in making questions
- Probing questions
- Higher order questions
- Divergent questions
- Recognising attending behaviour
- Illustrations and use of examples
- Lecturing
- Planned repetition
- Completeness

B. K. Passi (1976) described 13 skills in his book Becoming Better Teacher—Microteaching Approach. The different skills are as under:

- Writing Instructional Objectives
- Introducing a Lesson
- Fluency in Questioning
- Probing Questions
- Explaining
- Illustrating with Examples
- Stimulus Variation
- Silence and Non-verbal Cues
- Reinforcement
- Increasing Pupil Participation
- Using Blackboard
- Achieving Closure
- Recognising Attending Behaviour

List of Probable Teaching Skills for Different Stages of a Lesson

Planning Stage

(i) Writing Instructional Objectives

(ii) Selecting the Content

(iii) Organising Content

(iv) Selection of Audio Visual Aids Material

Introductory Stage

(i) Creating Set Induction

(ii) Introducing the Lesson

Presentation Stage

The presentation stage has four sub-stages. Each sub-stage needs different type of teaching skills which are given below:

Questioning Skills

(*i*) Structuring Classroom Questions

(*ii*) Fluency in Asking Questions

(*iii*) Probing Questions

(*iv*) Question—Delivery and Distribution

(*v*) Higher Order Questions

(*vi*) Divergent Questions

(*vii*) Responses Management

Presentation Skills

(*i*) Pacing of the Lesson

(*ii*) Lecturing

(*iii*) Explaining Discussing

(*iv*) Illustration with Examples

(*v*) Discussing

(*vi*) Demonstrating

Aid Using Skills

(*i*) Using Teaching Aids

(*ii*) Using Blackboard

(*iii*) Stimulus Variation

(*iv*) Silence and Non-verbal Cues

(*v*) Reinforcement Managerial Skills.

Managerial Skills

(*i*) Promoting Pupil Participation

(*ii*) Recognising Attending Behaviour

(*iii*) Management of the Class

(*iv*) Closing Stage

The stage includes the following skills:

(*i*) Achieving Closure

(*ii*) Planned Repetition

(iii) Giving Assignments

(iv) Evaluating the Pupils Progress

(v) Diagnosing pupil learning difficulties and remedial measure

INTEGRATION OF TEACHING SKILLS

Integration of teaching skills may be defined as a process of selection, organisation and utilisation of different teaching skills to form an effective pattern for realising the specified instructional objectives in a given teaching-learning situation.

According to Jangira and Ajit Singh: "Integration is the process through which a student-teacher acquires the ability to perceive with precision the teaching situation in its entirety, select and organise the teaching skills in the desired sequence to form effective patterns for realising the specified instructional objectives and use them with easy and fluency."

The teachers under training are given practice in the mastery of the different skills, then they are sent to the schools in real classroom situations where they are required to teach A question arises—should those teachers be given training for the integration of the different skills or not?

There are two groups of opinion which come forward with their agreements on the above said question. One group is of the opinion that some training for the integration of different skills is a must while the other group of thinkers opine that there is no need. They say that the teachers are able to integrate different skills automatically. The decided opinion is that the different teaching skills have to be integrated by using a number of strategies which are explained below:

Strategies for Integration of Skills

Vicarious Integration

In this type of integration, the pupil teacher is sent from microteaching setting to real classroom situation directly. In between, no special training for the integration of various skills is given to him. He is able to integrate the different skills in his own way as per his own desires and requirements.

Summative Strategy

After the lesson, teacher has mastered a few skills of teaching in microteaching, he is provided with another microteaching setting where he learns the integration of skills already learnt by him. The duration of time is increased for this type of lesson. If the practicing teacher has learnt two skills (S_1 and S_2) then he will learn the integration of those two skills. If he has learnt four skills($S_1+S_2+S_3+S_4$),he will integrate those four skills ($S_1+S_2+S_3+S_4$).The training for the integration of skills is provided in a controlled setting. Increase in the length of the lesson will require increase in the duration of time. Each lesson is observed and feedback is provided till the learner teacher is able to have a reasonable mastery in the integration of skills. Thus, the pupil teacher is sent to the real classroom situation in due course of time.

Additive Strategy

In this strategy, the pupil-teacher is given training for the mastery of two skills. Then, he learns integration of those two skills. After this, training for the third skill is given and then he learns integration of the third skill into the two already acquired. Thus, he goes on adding the newly learnt skill into the ones already learnt by him. Here, the time duration is increased as the length of the lesson increases.

Example: Suppose the pupil-teacher has learnt the skill of questioning and skill of reinforcement. He is then given training for the integration of those two skills. Thereafter he learns the third skill of stimulus variation and integrates that in the two already learnt.

Cluster Strategy

Cluster means a chunk or a group. The teacher combines together, let us suppose two skills—S_1 and S_2 in one lesson. Then, he learns in another lesson say three skills S_3, S_4 and S_5. After this he combines the above two clusters of five skills

(S_1+S_2+S_3+S_4+S_5)in a single lesson. In this way, he is learning the integration of skills. In one cluster at a time, he may choose any two or three skills as per his liking. In the second cluster again, he can pick up any skill or any number of skills. Whatever he learns in two clusters, then he combines the two and learns integration.

Diode Strategy

According to diode strategy, the pupil teacher learns the integration of two skills say S_1 and S_2. Then he learns the other two skills say S_3 and S_4. Thus, all the skills are learnt in pairs. Then they are integrated. This technique is actually in between the summative type and the additive type. Mastery over the skills is given in controlled setting. The learner teacher takes up two skills at a time as per his liking and convenience. After learning the skills in pairs, provided with real classroom teaching situation after he has learnt the skills and their integration.

Merits of Microteaching

In Indian context, microteaching can contain the following advantages over the traditional methods of learning the art of teaching:

1. In our traditional mode of teachers training a great dependence is observed on the availability of the pupils, classrooms and co-operation from the staff on the practising schools. The microteaching approach incorpor-ating simulating technique helps a training institution in overcoming the hardships faced on the task of organising student teaching for learning the art of teaching.
2. The Global concept of teaching is replaced by the analytical concept in microteaching approach. Her, complex task of teaching is looked upon as a set of simpler skills comprising specific classroom behaviours. This helps in the proper understanding of the meaning and concept of the term teaching.

3. Microteaching helps in reducing the complexities of the normal classroom teaching. It is a scaled down or miniature classroom teaching as it reduces the size of the class and duration of the lesson and provides proper opportunities for practicing one component teaching skill at a time by using single concept of the content.
4. In microteaching the student-teacher concentrate on practising a specific and well-defined teaching skill consisting of a set of teacher behaviours that are observable, controllable and practicable. Consequently microteaching provides more appropriate technique of learning the art of teaching than the traditional student teaching programme.
5. Microteaching helps in systematic and objective observation by providing specific observation schedule.
6. Microteaching works as a laboratory exercise to focus training on the acquisition of teaching skills and instructional techniques. Here a trainee can experiment with several alternatives in a limited time and resources. It is just like to learn the art of operating human body parts in a medical laboratory by a student doctor before actually operating a patient.
7. Microteaching provides economy in mastering the teaching skills. It saves the time and energy of the student-teacher as well as of the pupils. In microteaching it is not only easy for a student teacher to handle a micro-group (5-10 pupils) but also safe because they will have less problems of classroom discipline and subsequent mental tension as faced commonly in the traditional practice teaching programme. It also saves the pupils for being unnecessarily used as guinea pigs for training student teachers.
8. Another major advantage of microteaching lies in the provision of immediate, systematic, pin-pointed and objective feedback in behavioural terms. In the traditional teaching practice programme it is usually given in global

terms like 'improve hand writing', 'seek pupil's participation' etc., after the lapse of a lot of time.

9. Microteaching caters to the need of individual differences in the training of teachers. Her, an individual trainee may work for the development of teaching skills at his own rate depending on his teaching abilities.
10. Unlike traditional practice teaching programme it focuses attention on the modification of teacher behaviour and improvement of interaction process involved in the teaching-learning process.

In this way it is easily concluded that microteaching may be described as an effective, well-managed and controlled device of learning the art of teaching.

Demerits of Microteaching

1. Microteaching does not take into consideration the overall environment of teaching.
2. It is a skill-oriented technique instead of being content-oriented.
3. It has limited scope for developing the skills.
4. It does not provide broad based behaviours in terms of skills.
5. In training colleges, microteaching lab is very expensive.
6. It requires videotape recorder and other devices for making the micro-lesson very effective. It becomes difficult for training colleges to make such arrangements.
7. Experts in microteaching are generally scares.
8. It needs sufficient time to impart the teaching skills among all the student-teachers.
9. It is alone not enough to attain perfection in teaching. It will be effective if supported with interaction analysis and simulated teaching method.

Commissions and committees, from time to time have painted out the defects of teacher education programmes. There has been great criticism of teachers' training programmes by administrators and educators in our country. All agree that teacher's training programmes have failed to develop desirable teaching skills in perspective teachers. The teacher training programme has no impact on classroom teaching. Consequent upon the lack of efficiency and desirable skills in teachers, the quality of instruction is deteriorating year after year. Recent researchers in USA, UK and other advanced countries in classroom teaching have proved that classroom teaching may be objectively analysed and modified, according to the requirements, to develop desirable teaching skills and competencies in the student-teachers and even in in-service teachers.

Microteaching is one of the most recent innovations in teacher education programmes which aim to modify teacher's behaviour according to the specified objectives. Educationist in our country has recently recognised the importance of microteaching in preparing efficient classroom teacher.

Microteaching was developed only a decade ago, but in comparison with many other innovations in education, it has been adopted very quickly by many teacher educators in developed countries. However, its adoption in developing countries has been somewhat slower, mainly as a result of the notion that the use of laboratory systems, and in particular microteaching, is inherently dependent on the use of hardware and specially videotape recorders. Such equipment is very difficult to obtain in some developing countries both because of its relatively high cost and because of technical difficulties of operation and maintenance.

For microteaching one author has taken a wonderful and most relevant example, that is taking a teacher trainee to a school-classroom may be compared with taking a person, who has learnt the theory of swimming, to a river and asking him to swim. Will that person be able to swim and survive? Oh! No. It would rather be pitiable situation both for the person who is trying to learn swimming and the person who giving training in swimming. Taking the person to water for learning swimming is all right. But taking him to deep waters is not advisable at the early stages of learning. The person should be given training bit by bit, in knee deep water, say in water where the depth is 3 feet or so, then to 4 feet, 5 feet and so on.

This type of learning step by step, will prepare him well and then naturally his performance in deep waters will be all right. In the same way surgical doctor while under training performs minor operations first, then bigger ones. This type of learning step by step, easy things first and complicated and difficult ones afterwards, will ensure him a bright future with all success. This type of learning will encourage him all through. Things learnt first will become a sort of platform for him on the basis of which he will be learning far better things. Similarly, to become a good teacher or to teach in the school classroom the student teacher must get prior training for each skill so that by using these practised skill effective teaching can be made in classroom.

Research on Microteaching in India

A number of studies have been conducted in India on microteaching. Almost all the studies confirmed that microteaching is feasible and effective technique in training of teachers. The results of some of the studies are give below:

- Chaudsma (1974), found that microteaching was more effective than the traditional technique in the development of indirect teacher behaviour.
- Passi and Shah (1974) found that microteaching was effective in developing the skills of questioning, reinforcement, silence and non-verbal cues, illustration and use of examples. They further found the technique to be feasible. Student-teachers had developed favourable attitude towards the technique.
- Singh (1974) showed that microteaching was more effective technique as compared to interaction analysis and conventional approaches regarding modifications of teacher behaviour.

- A large scale experimental field-study was undertaken in 1975-76 by the Department of Teacher-Education, NCERT, New Delhi in collaboration with CASE, Baroda and nine colleges/University department of education. The main finding of the study is that the student-teachers trained through microteaching or modified micro-teaching technique display higher general teaching compared to the student-teachers trained under the traditional teacher training programme or the usual practice teaching programme.
- The major findings of the experimental field-study conducted by NCERT in collaboration with 22 institutions in 1976-77 are as follows:

  General teaching competence of student-teachers trained through microteaching with perceptual modelling does not differ with those trained under microteaching with either symbolic audio-modelling.

Background of the Study

Educational technology is a subject which provides techniques in education. In education many aspects play different role to impart the knowledge to the pupils. Among them teaching is the large base, which play a great job to educate the child. If teaching is effective, useful and understandable then only pupils get the knowledge and the objective of educating the children will be achieved by a teacher or educator.

Teaching constitute of many stages and skills, methods, tactics, techniques etc. If teaching skills are integrated and used in classroom then teaching becomes effective. So the student teacher should be trained to teach in classroom with different skills. All the skills together cannot be taught at once, so skills are presented one after another. The technique which gives the better way of teaching is "Microteaching". Before going to the classroom if microteaching training is provided to the student teachers definitely they perform very well in practice teaching. In this study the investigators have tried to know the use of microteaching and its impact on the student teachers and also tried to know how much the student teachers of Karnataka state know about microteaching and whether they are practicing it. Further, the study also encompasses the opinion of teacher educators towards use of microteaching and its impact on their student teachers. Now, the microteaching has become the part of the course of college of teacher education. Therefore, the investigators have studied different related research studies to get the direction for the present study. After studying all the researches the investigator gets idea to study about how much the student teachers know about Microteaching. How they use it and what is its impact on their teaching.

Improvement of Teachers' Skills Through Microteaching

Overview

This chapter deals with review of related studies. In this chapter the investigators have presented the relevant and related research studies pertaining to the problem. First, the Indian doctoral researches, then the foreign studies are given which is followed by the research articles from various journals and internet sources. Abstract of each study contains title/problem of the study, author's name, objectives, methodology and major findings of the study. Then the investigators have briefly synthesised and summarised all the studies and sharpened the problem of present study. This also provided the guidance to conduct and carryout the present study

Why Review of Related Studies?

Before commencement of the review of related studies, it is utmost important to know about the review of related studies. Review of related literature is defined as the study of literature which helps a research investigator to develop and design his own research methodology for conducting research by referring to literature in the form of journals, periodicals, abstract, reviews, monographs, handbooks, surveys and other resource books in the field of education.

A summary of the writings of recognised authorities and of previous research provides evidence that the researcher is familiar with what is already known and what is still unknown and untested. Since, effective research is based upon past knowledge, this step helps to eliminate the duplication of what has been done and provides useful hypotheses and helpful suggestions for significant investigation. Citing studies that show substantial agreement and those that seem to present conflicting conclusions helps to sharpen and define understanding of existing knowledge in the problem area, provides a background for the research project, and makes the reader aware of the status of issue.

The investigator should note certain important elements in searching related literature:

(i) Reports of studies of closely related problems that have been investigated.

(ii) A design of the study includes procedure employed and data gathering instruments used.

(iii) Populations that were sampled and sampling methods employed.

(iv) Variables that were defined.

(v) Faults that could have been avoided.

(vi) Recommendations for further studies.

Reasons for Review

The reasons for review of related literature are:

- To gain a background knowledge of research topic.
- To identify the concepts relating to it, potential relationships between them and to formulate researchable hypotheses.
- To identify appropriate methodology, research design, methods of measuring concepts and technique of analysis.
- To learn how others structured the reports.

Indian Studies

1. Dutta, Ram (1990) *Integration in Microteaching.*

In this study an attempt has been made to compare the effects of integration training with those of microteaching and traditional teaching programme.

The objectives of the study were to study the effect of microteaching on the GTC and attitude towards teaching of the experimental group and to study the effect of integration training to the additive model on QTC and attitude towards teaching of E2.

In this methodology the sample comprised 30 B.Ed. students divided into three sub-groups namely control group and experimental group E1 and E2. 10 students per group, each matched on five criterion variables i.e. age, sex, academic qualifications, general teaching competency scores and attitude towards teaching were considered in the study. The tools used included Baroada General Teaching Competence (BGTC), Rating Scale of Passi and Lalith; Teaching Attitude Inventory of Ahluwalia and College road.

In the major finding the traditional teaching techniques, the microteaching technique and integration training through the additive pattern had a significant and positive effect in developing General Teaching Competence and Traditional Training had a negative effect in developing attitude towards teaching. The microteaching technique had a positive effect in developing attitude towards teaching. Both microteaching technique and integration of skills through the additive pattern were found superior to the traditional technique and equally effective in developing general teaching competence.

2. Dwivedi, Jagdishwarr (1988), *An investigation into the effectiveness of microteaching in the development of psychomotor skills in biology practicals.*

This study attempts to investigate the effectiveness of microteaching in the development of psychomotor skills in biology practical.

The objective of the study was to find out the effectiveness of microteaching (the integrated and the non-integrated approach) in the acquisition of psychomotor skills.

The randomised control group pre-test and post-test experimental design was used. Experimental and control groups of equal numbers were made out. The two experimental groups were taught through the microteaching integrated and the non-integrated approach, other groups through approach. The control group was taught using two variations—one with the integrated and the other through the non-integrated traditional approach.

Four or three or two cycles of the Microteaching Integrated Approach (MTIA) contributed to the learning of the psychomotor skills of collecting, mounting and preserving as well as dissectional skills.

3. Gandhi, K. A. (1992), *Microteaching Approach for Student-Teachers.*

The study examines whether the development of teaching skills through microteaching approach helped in shaping behavioural modifications of student-teachers.

The objectives were to study whether the development of teaching skills through the microteaching strategy helped in shaping behaviour modification of students and to compare the outcomes with those acquired by the traditional approach.

In this methodology the sample comprised 40 students of B.Ed. They were divided into two groups of 20 each. Only 5 skills were taken into account. For each skill the concept was first explained to the whole group, and for each skill, a model lesson was given. Each trainee gave two micro-lessons in the simulated condition. The control group gave two traditional type lessons of 35 minutes duration in the real classroom setting. Flander's Interaction Analysis Categories (FIACs) and their communication in classroom was measured. Chi-square test was used as statistical tools.

Major findings were as compared to the student teachers trained through the microteaching approach, the student-teachers trained through the traditional approach *(i)* were more direct in their classroom verbal-behaviour *(ii)* employed a large percentage of teacher talk in the classroom behaviour and *(iii)* showed a narrower percentage of student-talk in their classroom behaviour.

4. Gor, Kantilal Visanji (1992), *A study of the effectiveness of microteaching strategies for developing the teaching competency of primary teacher-trainees.*

The objectives of the study were to study the effectiveness of microteaching strategies with respect to symbolic modelling and perceptual modelling upon attitude towards profession (PTAT Part 1), Professional Information (PTAT Part II) and interest in the teaching profession (PTAT Part III) of teacher trainees and to study the effectiveness of microteaching strategies in developing general teaching competency and attitude towards Microteaching.

In this methodology thirty-six teacher-trainees were selected to form two experimental group and eighteen teacher-trainees were selected to form the control group. Four separate book-lets for four specific skills were prepared by the researcher using the Advance Organiser Model. The tools used to collect the data were Primary Teachers Aptitude Test, Bhatt Group Test of intelligence in Gujrati etc.

The major findings were the perceptual modelling approach was significantly more effective than the symbolic modelling in developing the teaching competency of primary teacher-trainees. The symbolic modelling approach and perceptual modelling approach were significantly more effective than the traditional approach in developing the teaching competency of primary teacher trainees.

5. Bhattacharjee, R. (1981), *Effectiveness of microteaching in Developing Teaching Competence.*

The objectives of the project were to observe the effect of integration a few selected teaching skills upon the teaching competence of B.Ed. trainees.

Four skills were selected. A sample of 20 B.Ed. trainees was selected from one training college in Shillong, and divided into two equal groups in terms of age, sex, qualification etc. In both the groups each trainee was given two lessons in school setting and his performance was assessed through GTCS and ITCS. The obtained score was treated as pre-test score. Then, for experimental group the above four skills oriented and demonstrated. Again, in both the groups each individual gave two lessons (experimental group gave using four skills and control group members gave with traditional method) and again by using GTCS and ITCS were used to assess the performance. t-test was used to measure the statistics.

The study revealed that training for the integration of the four selected skills under the 'summative model' of integration had contributed to the teaching competence of the experimental group significantly in comparison with the control group.

6. Naik, V. V., (1984), *A Comparative Study of the Effect of Microteaching and Conventional Approach of Teacher Training upon Pupil's Achievement, Pupils' Perception and General Teaching Competence of Pre-service Student Teachers.*

The objectives of the study were to study the differential effect of microteaching and conventional teacher training approaches in relation to the achievement of pupils and to study the pupils' perception of student-teachers trained through microteaching and conventional teacher training approach.

The design envisaged two groups of student-teachers and pupils, one serving as the experimental and the other as the control group. The microteaching training was given to experimental group and the conventional teacher training was given to the control group. The sample consisted of 644 student-teachers and 620 eighth standard pupils. The data were collected by means of questionnaire and lesson. The tools employed in this study were Evaluation Schedules, General Teaching Competence Scale etc.

The major findings of the study were for total gain in achievement in physics, the experimental group scored significantly higher than the control.

7. Bhatia, S. K., *Microteaching with and without Integration Training using Additive Dimension with Peer Supervisor Feedback under Simulated and Real Conditions.*

The objectives of the study were to study the effectiveness of training through microteaching with skill integration intervention employing additive strategy and without skill integration intervention on the general teaching competence of in-service commerce teachers and also on the retention of general teaching competence, acquisition of the skills of reinforcement, probing questioning, illustrating with examples.

The tools used in the study were the Baroada General Teaching Competence scale, Ahluwalia's Teacher Attitude Inventory etc.

The important findings of the study were the treatment of skill integration interventions employing additive strategy administered to the experimental group and treatment of microteaching without skill integration intervention administered to the experimental group and treatment of microteaching without skill integration intervention administered to the control group significantly improved the general teaching competence of in-service commerce teacher at post-training stages.

8. Kalyanpurkar, S., *The effect of microteaching on the teaching competence of In-service Teachers and its impact on pupil's attainment and pupils' liking.*

The objectives were to study the effect of microteaching training on the development of selected skills, to study the effect of microteaching training on the development of general teaching competence of in-service teachers, to study the effect of microteaching training on the development of general teaching competence. To study the effect of microteaching treatment on pupil's attainment and pupil's retention and to study the effect of microteaching treatment on pupil likes for their teachers.

The hypotheses were: There would be no significant difference between post-test mean skill scores of the experimental and control groups. There would be no significant difference between post-test mean skill scores of the experimental and control groups. There would be no significant difference between post-test mean and GTC scores of the experimental and control groups when adjusted for pre-test GTC scores. The sample included 36 teachers and their 720 pupils from 17 schools. The pre-test, post-test control, experimental group design was employed in this study. The general teaching competence was measured with the help of General Teaching Competence Scale developed by Passi and Lalitha.

Raven's Standard Progressive Matrices were used to obtain a measure of pupils' mental ability score. The test-retest reliability co-efficient varied from 0.83 to 0.93. The data were analysed with the help of analysis of covariance The Findings were:

- Microteaching treatment had a positive significant effect on the development of skills.
- Microteaching treatment had a positive significant effect on the development of GTC, when the post-test GTC means of the two groups were adjusted for pre-test GTC scores.
- Microteaching treatment had a positive significant impact on pupils' attainment as well as on pupil's retention in the attainment.
- Microteaching treatment had positive significant impact on pupils' liking for their teachers when the means of the two groups were adjusted for scores.

Foreign Studies

1. Dave, C.S. (1987), *Relative effectiveness of microteaching having the summative model of integration versus the mini-*

teaching model in terms of general teaching competence, teacher attitude towards teaching, pupil-liking and pupil achievement.

The objectives of the study were to compare the effectiveness of summative model of integration the mini-teaching model of integration and traditional model of integration, in terms of general teaching competence, pupil achievement and attitude of teacher towards teaching.

The methodology was a pre-test, post-test parallel group design with one control group was followed. The student teachers of experimental Group 1 were trained with the help of mini-teaching model; Experimental Group II was trained with the summative model and the Control Group received training on a model of integration. Different tools like General Teaching Competence Scale, Personal Information Performa, Indore Teaching Assessment scale etc., were used to collect data. Statistical techniques like mean, SD, ANCOVA and t-test were used for analysis of the data.

Major finding of the study were the mini-teaching integration model was found superior to the summative-integration model of integration and traditional model of integration, in terms of development of general teaching competence in the student teachers. There was a significant effect of the mini-teaching model of integration in comparison to the summative model of integration and the traditional model of integration treatment on the achievement of pupils.

2. Cliff, J.C. and Others (1980), "A Cost Effectiveness Study of the Use of microteaching in the Education of Teachers." *British Journal of Educational Technology,* Vol. II, Issue 2, May 1980.

This report presents a cost-effectiveness model for pre-service and in-service teacher training in Australia, using a microteaching technique, relating educational (student-centred) factors and cost (management-centred) factors. The report is divided into four parts: *(i)* a literature survey and the experimental study; *(ii)* attachments to Part A; *(iii)* a selected bibliography on Microteaching; *(iv)* additional supporting material. Part A, Section one is devoted to the development of an experimental microteaching model, and presents an investigation of microteaching and a literature survey as background for the present research; planning, development and implementation of and experimental programme; design and data analysis of the programme; a study of transfer effects from training to classroom practice; development of a cost-model and discussion of general-cost estimates obtained from the model; a considered micro-teaching role in in-service programmes and a summary of findings. Part A, Section Two, presents an instrument for the measurement of skill attainment and details of a costing model and its use in costing a microteaching programme. Part B, attachments, presents *(i)* handouts to student-teachers describing the microteaching the microteaching programmes, *(ii)* a description of the Monash (Victoria) self-instructional, in-service training programme in technical teaching skills. *(iii)* the transcripts of three in-service tape-recording on low-order questions, high order questions, and use of identification probing and redirection questions, Part C of the report presents an annotated bibliography of microteaching, including seven bibliographies, nine reviews 451 general references and 86 annotations. Part D, Additional supporting material presents a survey on the use of micro-teaching in teacher training institutions within the Greater Melbourne Area, and a report on a Seminar on the development and implementation of microteaching at Melbourne University.

3. Ameena Ebraheem Al-Methan, "Merits of microteaching as perceived by Student-Teachers at Kuwait University". *Journal Pendidikan* 28 (2003)

The role of microteaching in teacher education programmes has been widely recommended by several educators. Some educators believe that the introduction of microteaching training is based on the shortcomings of the traditional teacher education programmes. Microteaching enables the pre-service student teachers to receive more training before starting their student teaching programmes.

The objectives of the study are:

- To construct a microteaching inventory which indicates the merits of microteaching as perceived by the student-teachers;
- To assess student teachers' perception on the merits of microteaching using the inventory.

The sample consisted of 75 science student teachers who were engaged in the construction of the microteaching inventory. The inventory was later tested on 67 trainee's majority in Science and Mathematics at the College of education.

- Student teachers were trained on microteaching through the infusion of microteaching training into the teaching method courses.
- A microteaching inventory was constructed based on the trainees' experience with the microteaching training process.
- Student teachers responses were gauged using the microteaching inventory.

Prior to the Microteaching, student teachers followed the theoretical aspects of microteaching for eight weeks after which students were given the opportunity to practice microteaching which was carried out for six weeks which involved three phases as follows:

1. Five-day observation and evaluation training;
2. Two-week microteaching training;
3. Three-week videotaping analysis and evaluation.

In the result and discussion the investigator has given tables for the characteristics and behaviours which trainees regarded as significant in describing the merits of Microteaching. Percentages of the total sample agreeing or strongly agreeing to *(i)* trainee's planning skills, *(ii)* personality and *(iii)* teaching competencies.

With regards to planning skills the majority of the trainees consider that microteaching training has equipped them with successful planning skill competencies namely designing of relevant teaching strategies, designing instruction to accommodate the different abilities of students, preparing relevant questions to be given to students and the ability to acquire basic or essential information needed to be taught.

When trainees were allowed to express their own attitudes of the merits of microteaching training, they asserted that the training has affected their personality in terms of attitude and classroom management. The effect of micro-teaching training on trainees' attitude is displayed by inviting students' point of view, encouraging student's enquiry, encouraging active participation, encouraging interpretations of observed data and accepting students' constructive ideas.

Trainees have spelled out the merits of microteaching in terms of equipping them with a very valuable quality, that is monitoring student progress by giving questions after every teaching objective, providing students with imperative feed-back and choosing both volunteers and non-volunteers to answer questions.

Finding suggests that through microteaching trainees would be able to demonstrate important teaching competencies.

Microteaching has proved to have a positive effect on the teaching quality of trainees. However, with regard to the findings of this study, it would be of interest if a follow-up study would be carried out to see how much of those qualities would really help student teachers during their student teaching in a regular teaching situation. As microteaching has greatly benefited teacher trainees it will continue to be an important and crucial component of teacher training.

4. Julie Gess–Newsome, Norman G. Lederman, *The pre- service microteaching course and science teacher's instructional decisions: A qualitative analysis.*

The purpose of this investigation was to qualitatively investigate the effects of a microteaching course on pre-service science teachers' perceptions of teaching, instructional decisions and changes in beliefs which occur throughout the course. A total of 17 pre-service teachers constituted the sample for this investigation. In addition to viewing and self-critiquing the video-tapes of their lessons. Students received both oral and written feedback from peers and instructors. Subject was also required to complete a reaction questionnaire concerning their beliefs/perceptions prior to the first presentation as well as following each of the four required presentations. Systematic comparisons among students' self-critique and reaction questionnaire yielded a total of 12 categories of concern/beliefs about teaching. These categories pertained to either "concerns for self" or "concerns for students". Although the subjects appeared to proceed through a develop-mental process beginning with concerns for self and moving toward concerns for students, analyses of subjects' comments about students revealed that such remarks were actually egocentric. Additionally the data indicated that pre-service teachers view planning as a complex, two-component process.

5. Nancy D. Bell, *Microteaching: what is it that is going on here?*

Although microteaching has been found to be an effective way of helping pre-service teachers learn about what it means to teach and while students themselves find it useful, researchers have not yet examined the task itself to discover exactly what it means to "micro-teach", then the purpose of this study was to learn more about the interactional structure of the task. The results of discourse analysis that was performed on 22 video-tapes of microteaching showed that the question of how to frame the task was a constant challenge to the students, who must simultaneously negotiate the roles of teacher, student, classmate and peer/friends. Analysis of the tapes as well as of questionnaire in which participants described their perception of the activity and explained how they approached the task, reveals that microteaching resembles "performance" or "classroom task" to a much greater extent that it does "teaching".

Summary of the Related Studies

In the above related studies the main objectives were to study the effect of microteaching, effectiveness of microteaching, to study the development of teaching skills through the microteaching strategy helped in shaping behaviour modification of students, effects of different types of microteaching etc.

In methodology the sample taken for the study were student teachers, and the tools used were GTCS, PIP, observation schedule, questionnaire etc.

The major findings of most of the studies indicate that the microteaching technique had a significant and positive effect on student teachers. It is also evident that the student teachers who get training of microteaching teach well in comparison to those who are taught through traditional training method. Studies show that they integrate these microteaching skills in the class. Microteaching has proved to have a positive effect on the teaching quality of trainee teachers.

Research Strategy for Data Collection

In this chapter the investigators have written about the problem which is to be studied and objectives of the study. The investigators have framed one major hypothesis, 32 alternative minor hypotheses. The content of this chapter also elaborates population, sampling technique and instrumentation in which tools used and procedure of data collection and statistical techniques by adopting them to data analysis.

Problem of the Study

The clear defining of the problem is problem half solved. The problem to be investigated must be defined unambiguously for that will help to discriminate relevant data from the irrelevant ones. Defining a research problem properly and clearly is a crucial part of a research study and must in no case be accomplished hurriedly.

How to define a research problem is no doubt a Herculean task. However, it is a task that must be tackled intelligently to avoid the perplexity encountered in research operation.

The task of defining a research problem, very often, follows a sequential pattern—the problem is stated in a general way, the ambiguities are resolved, thinking and rethinking process results in a more specific formulation of the problem so that it may be a realistic one in terms of the available data and resources and is also analytically meaningful. All this results in a well-defined research problem that is not only meaningful from an operational point of view, but is equally capable of paving the way for the development of working hypotheses and for means of solving the problem itself.

The statement of the problem is a declarative statement but may be in question form. This attempt to focus on a stated goal given direction to the research process.

The statement of the problem is, "To study the impact of microteaching on student-teachers of colleges of education in Karnataka ".

Microteaching is gradually becoming the important part of teacher training institute, so in this study the investigators sought to know what is Microteaching, how to use it and what impact the microteaching was putting on the student teachers, with reference to the Karnataka State's Secondary Level Teacher Training institutes.

Objectives of the Study

- To study the impact of microteaching on student teacher.
- To study the use of microteaching in different colleges of Education in Karnataka State.
- To study the perception of microteaching by teacher educators.

Hypotheses

In the words of George A. Lundber, "A hypothesis is a tentative generalisation, the validity of which remains to be tested. In its most elementary stage the hypothesis may be very hunch, guess, imaginative data, which becomes the basis for action or investigation".

According to Webster, "A hypothesis is a proposition, 'condition or principle which is assumed, perhaps without belief; in order to draw out its logical consequences and by this method to 'test its accord with facts which are known or may be determine".

Rummel and Balline say, "A hypothesis is a statement capable of being tested and thereby verified or rejected."

Formulation of Hypotheses

The investigators have formulated the alternative major and alternative minor hypotheses.

Alternative Major Hypothesis

"There is a positive impact of microteaching on the student teachers of College of Education in Karnataka state."

Alternative Minor Hypotheses

1. The student teachers of Karnataka state are well versed with the meaning of Microteaching.
2. The student teachers of Karnataka state know the objectives of Microteaching.
3. The student teachers of Karnataka state know the main purpose of Microteaching.
4. The student teachers of Karnataka state can explain the different components of Microteaching.
5. The student teachers of Karnataka state practice the microteaching skills.
6. The student teachers of Karnataka state practice the micro-teaching cycle.
7. The student teachers of Karnataka state know the method of microteaching lesson plan.
8. The student teachers of Karnataka state involved in organisation of Microteaching.
9. The student teachers of Karnataka state observe the microteaching lesson plans by using observation schedule.
10. The student teachers of Karnataka state know the planning of Microteaching.
11. The student teachers of Karnataka state know the importance of feedback.

12. The student teachers of Karnataka state get the demonstration of microteaching skills.
13. The student teachers of Karnataka state think that microteaching cycle should be introduced compulsorily to the student-teachers of B.Ed. course.
14. The student teachers of Karnataka state feel it is necessary for teacher educators of B.Ed. to demonstrate all the skills of Microteaching.
15. The student teachers of Karnataka state do not face difficulty in demonstrating microteaching skills.
16. The teacher educators of Karnataka state do not feel that training through microteaching is laborious for both student-teachers and their supervisors.
17. The teacher educators of Karnataka state do not feel that training through microteaching is time-consuming technique.
18. The teacher educators of Karnataka state feel that training through microteaching improves the practicing skills of student-teachers.
19. The teacher educators of Karnataka state feel that microteaching helps in improving teaching competency.
20. The teacher educators of Karnataka state think that observation play an important role in Microteaching.
21. The teacher educators of Karnataka state think that feedback helps in improving the skills.
22. The teacher educators of Karnataka state think that audio-video recording tools are good for feedback.
23 The teacher educators of Karnataka state think that microteaching gradually teaches integration of various teaching skills.
24. The teacher educators of Karnataka state do not feel that student-teachers feel boredom during practice of teaching skills.

25. The teacher educators of Karnataka state agree that their student teachers practice microteaching skills in accordance with microteaching cycle.
26. The teacher educators of Karnataka state agree that their student teacher perform the microteaching enthusiastically.
27. The teacher educators of Karnataka state teach minimum of 6 microteaching skills to their students.
28. The teacher educators of Karnataka state agree that student teachers practice at least 6 microteaching skills.
29. The teacher educators of Karnataka state do not think that student teachers want to go to practice teaching directly without undergoing Microteaching.
30. The teacher educators of Karnataka state think that the student-teacher trained through microteaching has positive significant academic impact in the classroom teaching.
31. The teacher educators of Karnataka state feel that microteaching increases the trainees' confidence in their own teaching abilities.
32. The teacher educators of Karnataka state agree that microteaching helps in preparing a good teacher.

Population

A population is an group of individuals that have one or more characteristics in common that are of interest to the researcher. Here, in this study population is all student teachers studying in secondary level teacher training institute of Karnataka state.

Sample

A sample is a small population selected for observation and analysis. By observing the characteristics of the sample, one can make certain inferences about the characteristics of the population from which it is drawn.

Sampling technique used: In Karnataka state there are 360 colleges of Education for Secondary School Teacher Training. There are four revenue divisions in Karnataka state, the investigators attempted for representative samples from each division. The investigators used purposive random sampling method and among these 4 divisions the investi-gators have chosen 22 colleges of Education randomly. The following table 3.1 indicates the number of college of Education taken for sampling.

Table 3.1 Indicating Sample of Study

S.No.	Division	No. of Colleges of Education Selected
1	Belgaum	13
2	Gulbarga	5
3	Bangalore	3
4	Mysore	1

The total sample taken for the study contains 220 student teachers and 44 teacher educator from different secondary level teacher training institutes of Karnataka state.

Tools

The investigators have prepared the questionnaire for student teachers and opinionnaire for teacher educators as the tools of the study. First the investigators prepared 60 items for questionnaire and 24 items for opinionnaire then gave it to the guide. After editing by the guide the tools were given to expert educationist like Deans and Professors of education and other research experts. The corrections suggested by the concerned academicians were incorporated and tools were administered on a small sample of student teachers and teacher educators from the host institution i.e. Maulana Azad National Urdu University, Hyderabad, where the investigators worked for standardisation of the tool. A sample of 50 student teachers and 10 teacher educators was used. The difficult item, double drum items or items with content errors were removed and simple items were replaced in consultation with the guide. The final questionnaire consisted of 36 items and was administered on the student teachers. The opinionnaire consisted of 20 items and it was administered on the teacher educators.

The questionnaire is made up of 36 different items which are divided in 12 sections of 3 items each.

Procedure of Data Collection

The investigators sent 10 questionnaires and 2 opinionnaires to each of the College of Education taken as sample by post. These questionnaires and opinionnaires were accompanied by the introduction letter of the guide and request letter of the investigators with detailed instructions. Further, a self-addressed stamped envelop was also placed for ensuring feedback from the concerned college. The investigators also followed the post through phone. The sampled institutions were asked to send the filled-in tools in the self-addressed stamped envelop sent by the investigators. Some of the institutes sent immediate feedback and some delayed it. A reminder and letter of gratitude was also sent to the concerned institutes. Further, interaction was made through phone to ensure more responses. This has helped the investigators to obtain feedback from most of the institutes. However, few of the institutes apologise for not responding as the vacation had commenced for the student teachers and who were not available for responding to the questionnaires. The investigators have conveyed gratitude to all the institutes for their concerned towards research in the field of education.

Statistical Techniques

The investigators made use of computer extensively for analysis of the data. The data was fed to the computer in the Microsoft office (MS Excel) sheet. The percentage analysis of positive and non-positive responses was made using the same application for each of the item in opinionnaires and categories of items (having three items in each category) for questionnaires. The response percentage, thus obtained was converted into graphical format and thereby bar graphs were prepared using these data. The investigators have also made use of black and white graphical presentations as this would give a pleasant look in the print and will be more clear for a reader. The conclusions were thus drawn from such analysis.

Present Scenario of Microteaching in the Light of Data

Overview

In this chapter the investigators have discussed about the procedure of data analysis. The investigators have selected each of the minor null hypotheses and percentage analysis of each of the item was done. The same has been indicated in graphical form. Lastly conclusion about the minor hypotheses is also drawn for different items. Then the investigators have elaborated the interpretations and conclusions.

NULL HYPOTHESES

Null Major Hypothesis

"There is no positive impact of microteaching on the student teachers of College of Education in Karnataka state."

Null Minor Hypotheses

1. The student teachers of Karnataka state are not well versed with the meaning of microteaching.
2. The student teachers of Karnataka state do not know the objectives of microteaching.
3. The student teachers of Karnataka state do not know the main purpose of microteaching.

4. The student teachers of Karnataka state cannot explain the different components of microteaching.
5. The student teachers of Karnataka state do not practice the microteaching skills.
6. The student teachers of Karnataka state do not practice the microteaching cycle.
7. The student teachers of Karnataka state do not know the method of microteaching lesson plan.
8. The student teachers of Karnataka state do not involve in organisation of microteaching.
9. The student teachers of Karnataka state do not observe the microteaching lesson plans by using observation schedule.
10. The student teachers of Karnataka state do not know the planning of microteaching.
11. The student teachers of Karnataka state do not know the importance of feedback.
12. The student teachers of Karnataka state do not get the demonstration of microteaching skills.
13. The teacher educators of Karnataka state do not think that microteaching cycle should be introduced compulsorily to the student-teachers of B.Ed. course.
14. The teacher educators of Karnataka state do not feel it necessary for teacher educators of B.Ed. to demonstrate all the skills of microteaching.
15. The teacher educators of Karnataka state face difficulty in demonstrating microteaching skills.
16. The teacher educators of Karnataka state feel that training through microteaching is laborious for both student-teachers and their supervisors.
17. The teacher educators of Karnataka state feel that training through microteaching is time consuming technique.
18. The teacher educators of Karnataka state do not feel that training through microteaching improves the practicing skills of student-teachers.

19. The teacher educators of Karnataka state do not feel that microteaching helps in improving teaching competency.
20. The teacher educators of Karnataka state do not think that observation play an important role in microteaching.
21. The teacher educators of Karnataka state do not think that feedback helps in improving the skills.
22. The teacher educators of Karnataka state do not think that audio-video recording tools are good for feedback.
23. The teacher educators of Karnataka state do not think that microteaching gradually teaches integration of various teaching skills.
24. The teacher educators of Karnataka state feel that student-teachers feel boredom during practice of teaching skills.
25. The teacher educators of Karnataka state do not agree that their student teachers practice microteaching skills in accordance with microteaching cycle.
26. The teacher educators of Karnataka state do not agree that their student teacher perform the microteaching enthusiastically.
27. The teacher educators of Karnataka state do not teach minimum of 6 microteaching skills to their students.
28. The teacher educators of Karnataka state do not agree that student teachers practice at least 6 microteaching skills.
29. The teacher educators of Karnataka state think that student teachers want to go to practice teaching directly without undergoing microteaching.
30. The teacher educators of Karnataka state do not think that the student-teacher trained through microteaching has positive significant academic impact in the classroom teaching.
31. The teacher educators of Karnataka state do not feel that microteaching increases the trainees' confidence in their own teaching abilities.

32. The teacher educators of Karnataka state do not agree that microteaching helps in preparing a good teacher.

ITEMWISE PERCENTAGE ANALYSIS

ITEMWISE PERCENTAGE ANALYSIS
FOR QUESTIONNAIRE

Null Minor Hypotheses 1

The student teachers of Karnataka state are not well versed with the meaning of microteaching.

A1: *Do you know the meaning of microteaching?*

A2: *Do you think mcroteaching is the type of simulated teaching?*

A3: *Do you know the definition of microteaching?*

Table 4.1: Data Show Responses for Meaning of Microteaching

Variable		Responses	A1	A2	A3
Gender	Female	Yes	100.00	92.38	96.19
		No	0.00	7.62	3.81
	Male	Yes	100.00	86.11	94.44
		No	0.00	13.89	5.56
Type of Institution	Govt.	Yes	100.00	94.59	100.00
		No	0.00	5.41	0.00
	Aided	Yes	100.00	90.00	90.00
		No	0.00	10.00	10.00
	Unaided	Yes	100.00	88.46	94.62
		No	0.00	11.54	5.38
Locality	Rural	Yes	0.00	0.00	0.00
		No	0.00	0.00	0.00
	Semi-Urban	Yes	100.00	89.29	89.29
		No	0.00	10.71	10.71
	Urban	Yes	100.00	89.93	96.94
		No	0.00	10.07	3.36
Stream of Degree	Arts	Yes	100.00	92.68	95.93
		No	0.00	7.32	4.07
	Science	Yes	100.00	83.33	94.44
		No	0.00	16.67	5.56
Total		Yes	100.00	89.83	95.48
		No	0.00	10.17	4.52

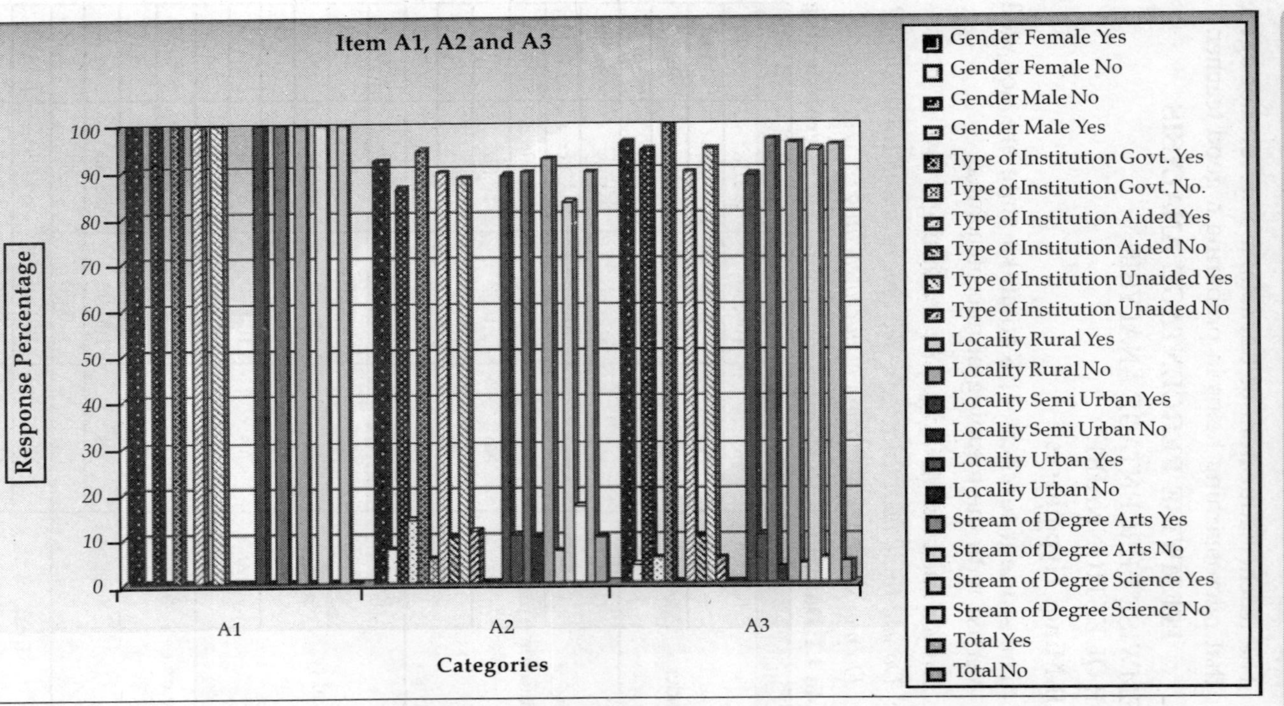

Graph 4.1: **Data Show Responses for Meaning of Microteaching**

The data in the table 4.1 revealed that 100 per cent respondents responded yes to the item A1. All male, female, government, aided, unaided, rural, semi-urban, urban, Arts and Science student teachers responded yes to the item which means all student teachers know the meaning of microteaching.

For item A2 92.38 per cent female and 86.11 per cent male responded yes, it indicates that more number of female student teachers know the meaning of microteaching than the males. 94.59 per cent government, 90 per cent aided, 88.46 per cent unaided student teachers responded yes, which means Government college student teachers know the meaning than the aided and unaided. 89.29 per cent semi-urban, 89.93 per cent urban student teachers responded yes, this point out that equal number of student teachers know the meaning from both the areas. 92.68 per cent arts, 83.33 per cent science student teachers responded yes and it means more number of arts student teachers know about the microteaching than the science student teachers and in total 89.83 per cent of the respondents responded yes which means most of the student teachers think microteaching is the type of simulated teaching.

For item A3 96.19 per cent female and 94.44 per cent male respondent responded yes, it means more female student teachers know the phases, 100 per cent government, 90 per cent aided, 94.62 per cent unaided student teachers responded yes, which indicates that all the government student teachers know the phases and more number of unaided student teachers know the phases than the aided, 89.29 per cent semi-urban, 96.64 per cent urban student teachers responded yes, more number of urban students know the phases than the semi-urban and 94.44 per cent arts, 95.48 per cent science student teachers responded yes which revealed that more science students know it than the arts student teachers and in total 95.48 per cent respondents responded yes which means most of the student teachers know the phases of microteaching.

By above all interpretation we can draw that the student teachers of Karnataka state know the meaning of micro-teaching, so the null minor hypothesis 1 is rejected and the alternative minor hypothesis 1 is accepted.

Null Minor Hypothesis 2

The student teachers of Karnataka state do not know the objectives of microteaching.

B1: *Do you know the objectives of microteaching?*

B2: *Do you agree with the statement, "Teachers are made, but not born"?*

B3: *Do you think that microteaching is helpful in classroom teaching?*

Table 4.2: Data Show Responses for Objectives of Microteaching

Variable		Responses	B1	B2	B3
Gender	Female	Yes	99.05	95.24	100.00
		No	0.95	4.76	0.00
	Male	Yes	91.67	90.28	90.28
		No	8.33	9.72	9.72
Type of Institution	Govt.	Yes	100.00	94.59	100.00
		No	0.00	5.41	0.00
	Aided	Yes	90.00	80.00	90.00
		No	10.00	20.00	10.00
	Unaided	Yes	95.38	93.85	95.38
		No	4.62	6.15	4.62
Locality	Rural	Yes	0.00	0.00	0.00
		No	0.00	0.00	0.00
	Semi-Urban	Yes	82.14	85.71	85.71
		No	17.86	14.29	14.29
	Urban	Yes	98.66	94.63	97.99
		No	1.34	5.37	2.01
Stream of Degree	Arts	Yes	98.37	94.31	99.19
		No	1.63	5.69	0.81
	Science	Yes	90.74	90.74	88.89
		No	9.26	9.26	11.11
Total		Yes	96.05	93.22	96.05
		No	3.95	6.78	3.95

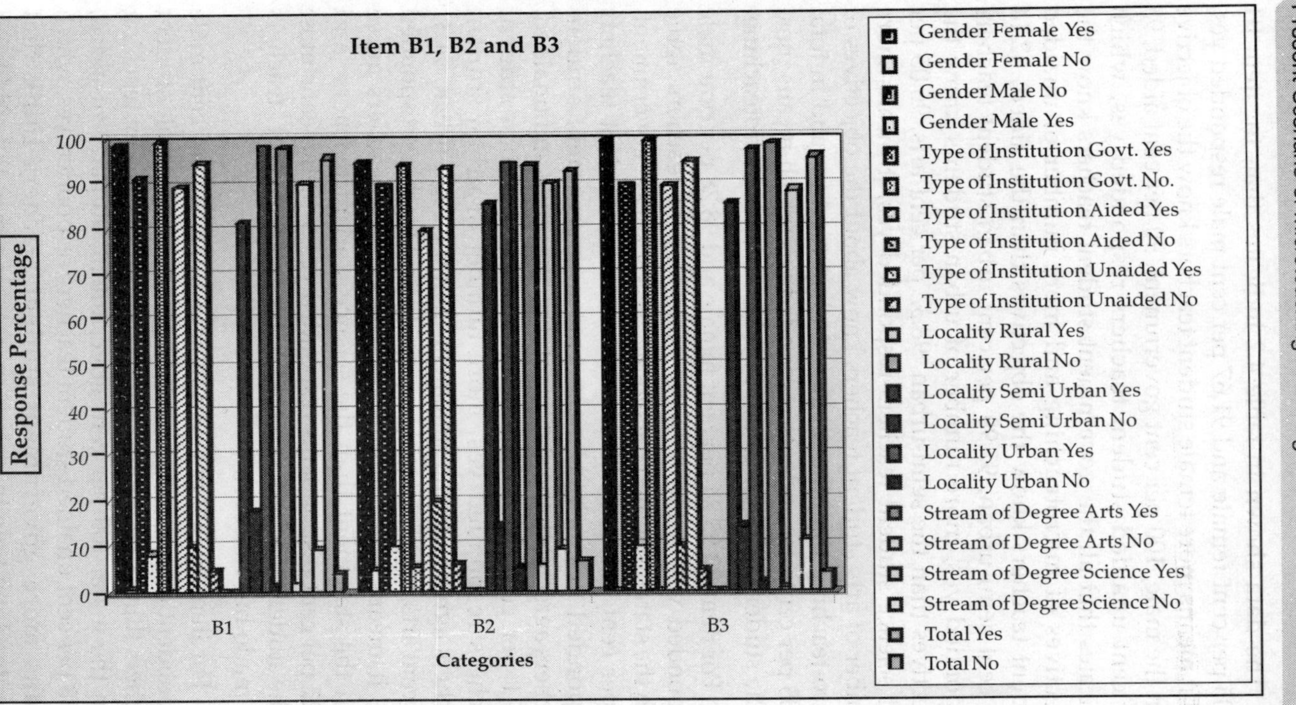

Graph 4.2: **Data Show Responses for Objectives of Microteaching.**

The data shown in table 4.2 indicates that, for item B1 99.05 per cent female and 91.67 per cent male responded yes, and it means more female student teachers know the objective than the male, 100 per cent government, 90 per cent aided, 95 per cent unaided student teachers responded yes, which indicates that all the government student teachers know the objectives of microteaching and more number of unaided student teachers know the objectives than the aided, 82.14 per cent semi-urban, 97.99 per cent urban student teachers responded yes, more number of urban students know the objectives than the semi-urban 98.37 per cent arts, 96.05 per cent science student teachers responded yes, it means more number of arts student teachers know about the objectives of micro-teaching than the science student teachers and in total 96.05 per cent respondents responded yes which means most of the student teachers know the objectives of microteaching.

For item B2 95.24 per cent female and 98.28 per cent male responded yes, it means more male student teachers agree with the statement than the female, 94.59 per cent government, 80 per cent aided, 93.85 per cent unaided student teachers responded yes, which means more government student teachers agree with the statement than the aided and unaided, 85.71 per cent semi-urban, 94.63 per cent urban student teachers responded yes, more number of urban student teachers agree with the statement than the semi-urban. 94.31 per cent arts, 93.22 per cent science student teachers responded yes, it means more number of arts student teachers agree with the statement than the science student teachers and 93.22 per cent respondents responded yes, which means most of the student teachers agree with the statement that "teachers are made but not born".

For item B3 100 per cent female and 90.28 per cent male respondent responded yes, which means more female student teachers think that microteaching helps in classroom teaching than the male, 100 per cent government, 90 per cent aided, 95.38 per cent unaided student teachers responded yes, which means more government student teachers think that microteaching help in classroom teaching than the aided and unaided, 85.71 per cent semi-urban, 97.99 per cent urban student teachers responded yes, more number of urban student teachers think that microteaching help in classroom teaching than the semi-urban and 99.19 per cent arts, 88.89 per cent science student teachers responded yes, it means more number of arts student teachers think that microteaching help in classroom teaching than the science student teachers and 96.05 per cent of respondents responded yes which means most of the student teachers think that microteaching help in classroom teaching

By above all interpretations it can be drawn that the student teachers of Karnataka state know the objectives of microteaching, so the null minor hypothesis 2 is rejected and the alternative minor hypothesis 2 is accepted.

Null Minor Hypothesis 3

The student teachers of Karnataka state do not know the main purpose of microteaching.

C1: *Do you know the purpose of microteaching?*

C2: *Do you feel that microteaching really improves your teaching skills?*

C3: *Do you think that microteaching improves classroom interaction?*

The data in table 4.3 indicates that, for the item C1 97.14 per cent female and 95.83 per cent male responded yes, which means more female student teachers know the purpose of microteaching than the male, 100 per cent government, 100 per cent aided, 96.15 per cent unaided student teachers responded yes, as compare to unaided government and aided student teachers are more who know the purpose of microteaching. 96.43 per cent semi-urban, 96.64 per cent urban student teachers responded yes, from both the area nearly equal student teachers know the purpose of microteaching, 96.75 per cent arts, 96.30 per cent science student teachers responded yes from both the streamline nearly equal student teachers know the purpose of microteaching, and in total 96.61 per cent respondents responded yes, which means most of the student teachers know the purpose of microteaching.

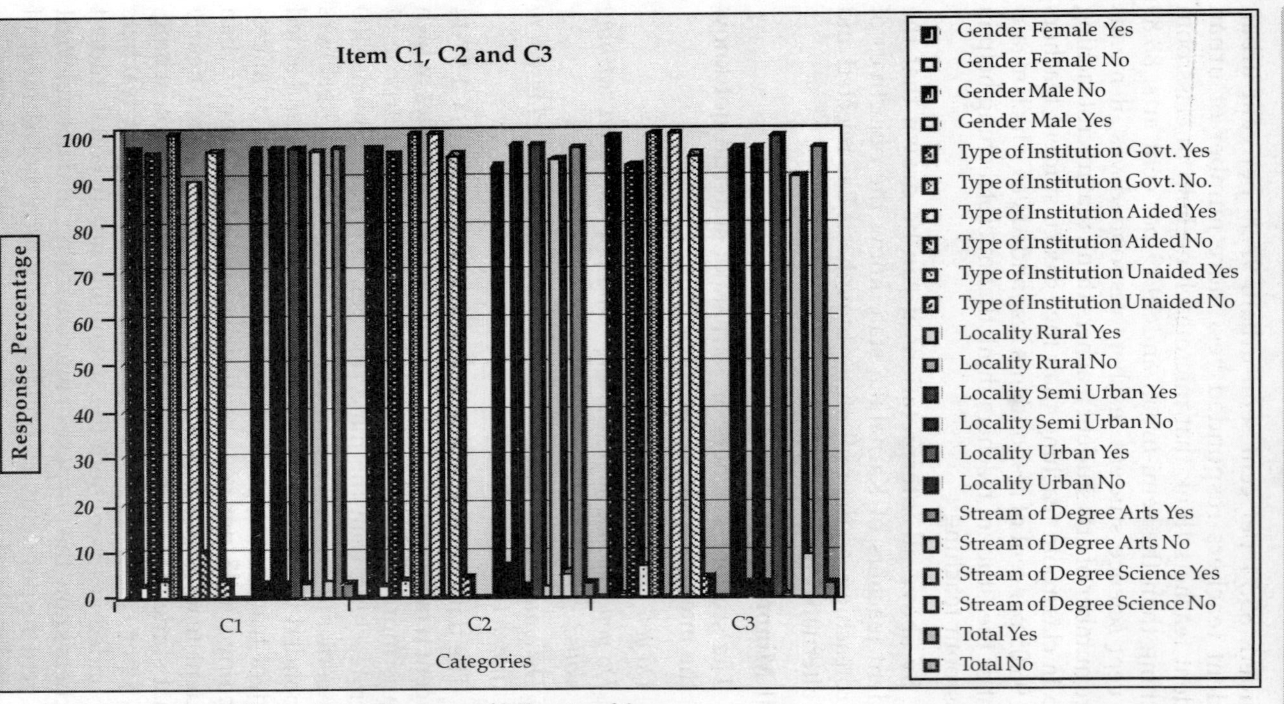

Graph 4.3: Data Show Views about Purpose of Microteaching

Table 4.3: Data Show Views about Purpose of Microteaching

Variable		Responses	C1	C2	C3
Gender	Female	Yes	97.14	97.14	99.05
		No	2.86	2.86	0.95
	Male	Yes	95.83	95.83	93.06
		No	4.17	4.17	6.94
Type of Institution	Govt.	Yes	100.00	100.00	100.00
		No	0.00	0.00	0.00
	Aided	Yes	90.00	100.00	100.00
		No	10.00	0.00	0.00
	Unaided	Yes	96.15	95.38	95.38
		No	3.85	4.62	4.62
Locality	Rural	Yes	0.00	0.00	0.00
		No	0.00	0.00	0.00
	Semi-Urban	Yes	96.43	92.86	96.43
		No	3.57	7.14	3.57
	Urban	Yes	96.64	97.32	96.64
		No	3.36	2.68	3.36
Stream of Degree	Arts	Yes	96.75	97.56	99.19
		No	3.25	2.44	0.81
	Science	Yes	96.30	94.44	90.74
		No	3.70	5.56	9.26
Total		Yes	96.61	96.61	96.61
		No	3.36	3.39	3.39

For item C2 97.14 per cent female and 95.83 per cent male responded yes, which means more female student teachers feel that microteaching really improves teaching skills than the male, 100 per cent government, 100 per cent aided, 95.38 per cent unaided student teachers responded yes, which means that all the student teachers from Government and aided feel that microteaching really improves teaching skills. They are more than the unaided student teachers 92.86 per cent semi-urban, 97.32 per cent urban student teachers responded yes, more number of urban student teachers feel that microteaching really improves teaching skills than the semi-urban, 97.56 per cent arts, 94.44 per cent science student teachers responded yes. It means more number of arts student teachers feel that microteaching really improves teaching skills than the science student teachers and in total 96.61 per cent respon-dents responded yes which means most of the student teachers feel that microteaching really improves your teaching skills.

For item C3 99.05 per cent female and 93.06 per cent male respondent responded yes, which means more female student teachers think that microteaching improves classroom interaction than the male, 100 per cent government, 100 per cent aided, 95.38 per cent unaided student teachers responded yes, which means that all the student teachers from Government and aided think that microteaching improves classroom interaction they are more than the unaided student teachers, 96.43 per cent semi-urban, 96.64 per cent urban student teachers responded yes, which indicates that from both the area nearly equal student teachers think that microteaching improves classroom interaction and 99.19 per cent arts, 96.61 per cent science student teachers responded yes, from both the strea-mline nearly equal student teachers think that microteaching improves classroom interaction and in total 96.61 per cent of respondents responded yes which means most of the student teachers think that microteaching improves classroom interaction.

By above all interpretations it can be drawn that the student teachers of Karnataka state know the, purpose of microteaching, so the null minor hypothesis 3 is rejected and the alternative minor hypothesis 3 is accepted.

Null Minor Hypothesis 4

The student teachers of Karnataka state cannot explain the different components of microteaching.

D1: *Do you know the components of microteaching skills?*

D2: *Do you understand the planning stage in microteaching?*

D3: *Do you know closing stage in microteaching?*

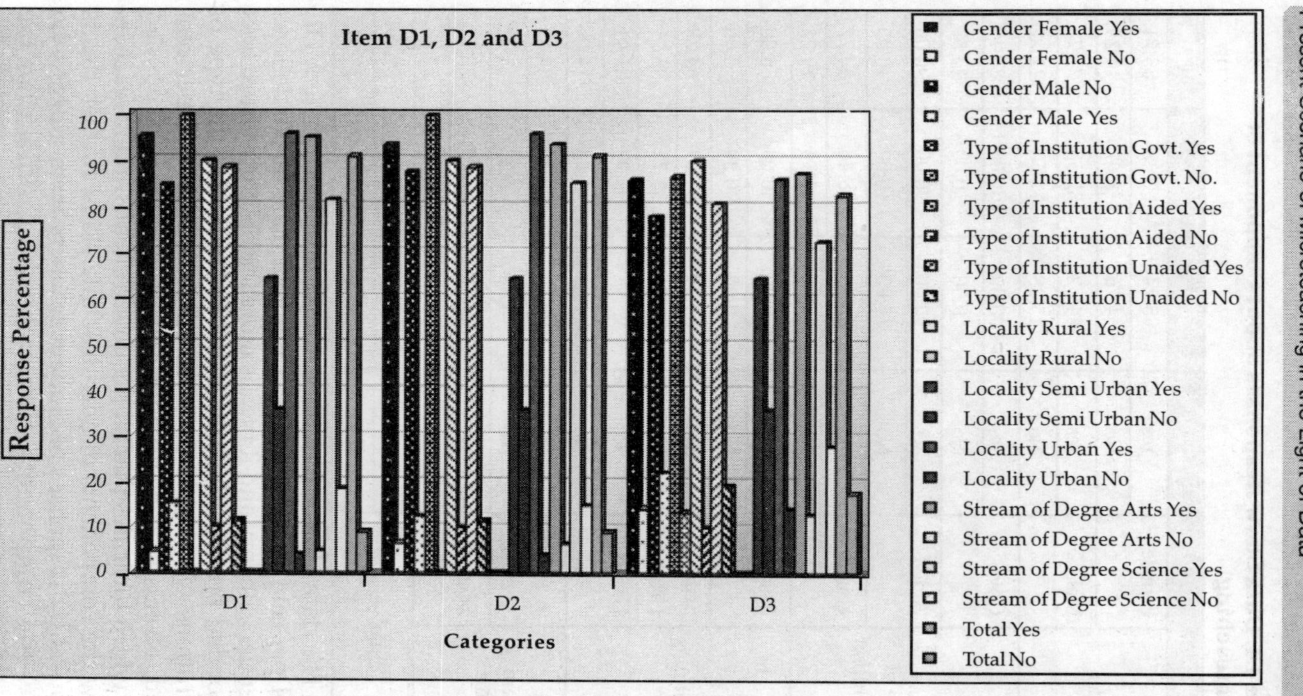

Graph 4.4: **Data Show Responses about Component of Microteaching**

Table 4.4: Data Show Responses about Component of Microteaching

Variable		Responses	D1	D2	D3
Gender	Female	Yes	95.24	93.33	85.71
		No	4.76	6.67	14.29
	Male	Yes	84.72	87.50	77.78
		No	15.28	12.50	22.22
Type of Institution	Govt.	Yes	100.00	100.00	86.49
		No	0.00	0.00	13.51
	Aided	Yes	90.00	90.00	90.00
		No	10.00	10.00	10.00
	Unaided	Yes	88.46	88.46	80.77
		No	11.54	11.54	19.23
Locality	Rural	Yes	0.00	0.00	0.00
		No	0.00	0.00	0.00
	Semi-Urban	Yes	64.29	64.29	64.29
		No	35.71	35.71	35.71
	Urban	Yes	95.97	95.97	85.91
		No	4.03	4.03	14.09
Stream of Degree	Arts	Yes	95.12	93.50	86.99
		No	4.88	6.50	13.01
	Science	Yes	81.48	85.19	72.22
		No	18.52	14.81	27.78
Total		Yes	90.96	90.96	82.49
		No	9.04	9.04	17.51

The data shown in table 4.4 indicates that, for item D1, 95.24 per cent female and 84.72 per cent male responded yes in gender category and it means more female student teachers responded positive than the male. Secondly, for the type of institutions viz., 100.00 per cent government, 90.00 per cent aided, 88.46 per cent unaided student teachers responded yes, which indicates that all the government student teachers know the components of microteaching skills, further, this is followed by responses of student teachers from aided, who know the components of microteaching skills than the remaining group from unaided.

Based on the locality the data indicates that 64.29 per cent semi-urban, 95.97 per cent urban student teachers responded yes. This indicates that more number of urban student teachers know the components of microteaching skills than their semi-urban counterparts. The data based on the degree stream show that 95.12 per cent arts, 81.48 per cent science student teachers responded yes. It is evident from the data that more number of arts student teachers know the components of microteaching skills than the science student teachers. The overall response data to this item shows that a total of 90.96 per cent respondents responded yes which means most of the student teachers know the components of microteaching skills.

For item D2, 93.33 per cent female and 87.50 per cent male responded yes in gender category and it means more female student teachers understand the planning stage in micro teaching than the male. Secondly, for the type of institutions viz., 100.00 per cent government, 90.00 per cent aided, 88.46 per cent unaided student teachers responded yes, which indicates that all of the government student teachers under stand the planning stage in microteaching, further, this is followed by responses of student teachers from aided unaided respectively. Based on the locality the data indicates that 64.29 per cent semi-urban, 95.97 per cent urban student teachers responded yes. This indicates that more number of urban student teachers understand the planning stage in microteaching than their semi urban counterparts. The data based on the degree stream show that 93.50 per cent arts, 85.19 per cent science student teachers responded yes. It is evident from the data that more number of arts student teachers understand the planning stage in microteaching than the science student teachers. The overall response data to this item shows that a total of 90.96 per cent respondents responded yes which means most of the student teachers understand the planning stage in microteaching.

For item D3, 85.71 per cent female and 77.78 per cent male responded yes in gender category and it means more female student teachers know closing stage in microteaching than the male. Secondly, for the type of institutions viz., 86.49 per cent government, 90.00 per cent aided, 80.77 per cent unaided student teachers responded yes, which indicates that most of the aided student teachers know closing stage in microteaching, further, this is followed by responses of student teachers from government, who know closing stage in microteaching than the remaining group from unaided. Based on the locality the data indicates that 64.29 per cent semi-urban, 85.91 per cent urban student teachers responded yes. This indicates that more number of urban student teachers know closing stage in microteaching than their semi-urban counterparts. The data based on the degree stream show that 86.99 per cent arts, 72.22 per cent science student teachers responded yes. It is evident from the data that more number of arts student teachers know closing stage in microteaching than the science student teachers. The overall response data to this item shows that a total of 82.49 per cent respondents responded yes, which means most of the student teachers know closing stage in microteaching.

From the above data/interpretations we can draw a conclusion that the student teachers of Karnataka state explain different components of microteaching, so the null minor hypothesis 4 is rejected and the alternative minor hypothesis 4 is accepted.

Null Minor Hypothesis 5

The student teachers of Karnataka state do not practice the microteaching skills.

E1: *Do you know how to use microteaching for practicing skills of teaching?*

E2: *Do you practice at least six microteaching skills?*

E3: *Do you know different skills of microteaching?*

The data shown in table 4.5 indicates that, for the item E1, 95.24 per cent female and 87.50 per cent male responded yes in gender category, it means more female student teachers

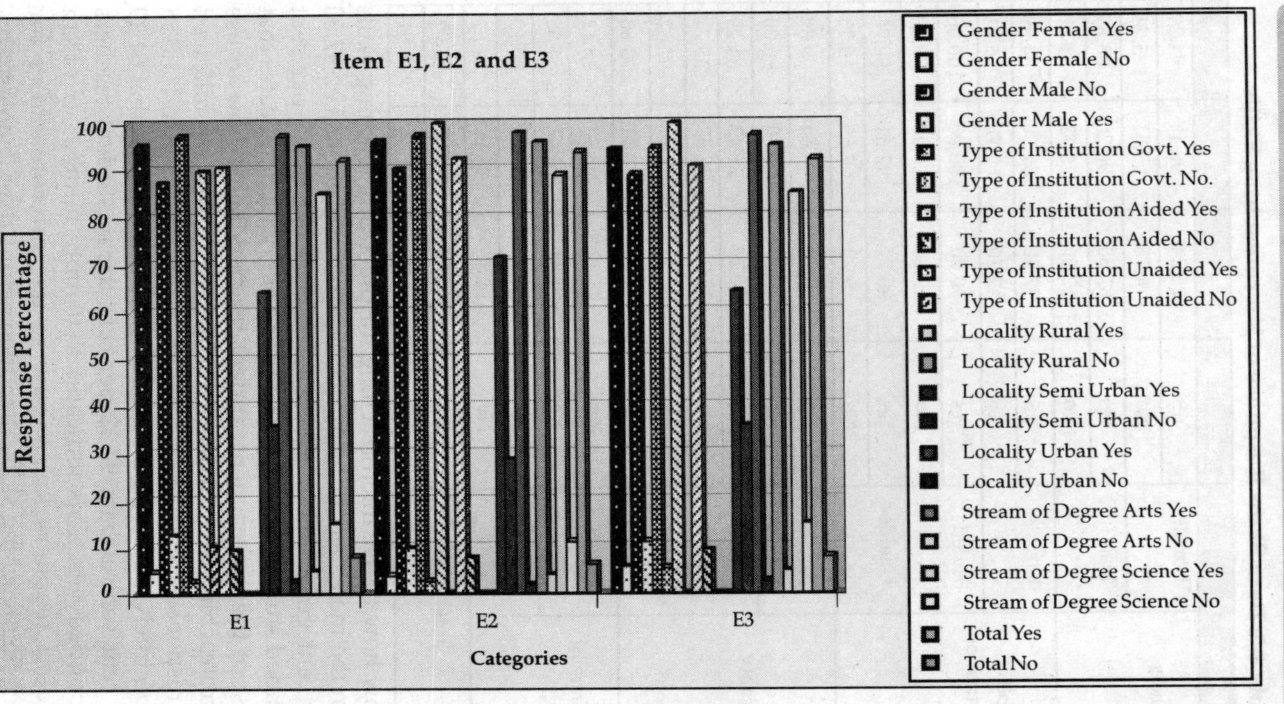

Graph 4.5: **Data Show Response of Microteaching Skills**

Table 4.5: Data Show Response of Microteaching Skills

Variable		Responses	E1	E2	E3
Gender	Female	Yes	95.24	96.19	94.29
		No	4.76	3.81	5.71
	Male	Yes	87.50	90.28	88.89
		No	12.50	9.72	11.11
Type of Institution	Govt.	Yes	97.30	97.30	94.59
		No	2.70	2.70	5.41
	Aided	Yes	90.00	100.00	100.00
		No	10.00	0.00	0.00
	Unaided	Yes	90.77	92.31	90.77
		No	9.23	7.69	9.23
Locality	Rural	Yes	0.00	0.00	0.00
		No	0.00	0.00	0.00
	Semi-Urban	Yes	64.29	71.43	64.29
		No	35.71	28.57	35.71
	Urban	Yes	97.32	97.99	97.32
		No	2.68	2.01	2.68
Stream of Degree	Arts	Yes	95.12	95.93	95.12
		No	4.88	4.07	4.88
	Science	Yes	85.19	88.89	85.19
		No	14.81	11.11	14.81
Total		Yes	92.09	93.79	92.09
		No	7.91	6.21	7.91

know how to use microteaching for practicing teaching skills than the male. Secondly, for the type of institutions i.e., 97.30 per cent government, 90.00 per cent aided, 90.77 per cent unaided student teachers responded yes, which indicates that most of the government student teachers know how to use microteaching for practicing teaching skills, which is followed by responses of student teachers from unaided and aided respectively. Based on the locality the data indicates that 64.29 per cent semi-urban, 97.32 per cent urban student teachers responded yes. This indicates that more number of urban student teachers know how to use microteaching for practicing teaching skills than their semi-urban counterparts.

The data based on the degree stream show that 95.12 per cent arts, 85.19 per cent science student teachers responded yes. It is evident from the data that more number of arts student teachers know how to use microteaching for practicing teaching skills than the science student teachers. The overall response data to this item shows that a total of 92.09 per cent respondents responded yes, which means most of the student teachers know how to use microteaching for practicing teaching skills.

For item E2, 96.19 per cent female and 90.28 per cent male responded yes in gender category, it means more female student teachers agree that they practice at least six microteaching skills more than the male. Secondly, for the type of institutions i.e., 97.30 per cent government, 100.00 per cent aided, 92.31 per cent unaided student teachers responded yes, which indicates that all of the aided student teachers practice at least six microteaching skills, which is followed by responses of student teachers from government and unaided respectively. Based on the locality the data indicates that 71.43 per cent semi-urban, 97.99 per cent urban student teachers responded yes. This indicates that all most all urban student teachers practice six microteaching skills in comparison with their semi-urban counterparts. The data based on the degree stream show that 95.93 per cent arts, 88.89 per cent science student teachers responded yes. It is evident from the data that more number of arts student teachers practice six skills than the science student teachers. The overall response data to this item shows that a total of 93.79 per cent respondents responded yes which means most of the student teachers practice at least six microteaching skills.

For item E3, 94.29 per cent female and 88.89 per cent male responded yes in gender category and it means more female student teachers know different skills of microteaching than the male. Secondly, for the type of institutions i.e., 94.59 per cent government, 100.00 per cent aided, 90.77 per cent unaided student teachers responded yes, which indicates that all of the aided student teachers know different skills of microteaching, which is followed by responses of student teachers from government and unaided respectively. Based on the locality the data indicates that 64.29 per cent semi-urban, 97.32 per cent urban student teachers responded yes. This indicates that more number of urban student teachers know different skills of microteaching than their semi-urban counterparts. The data based on the degree stream shows that 95.12 per cent arts, 85.19 per cent science student teachers responded yes. It is evident from the data that more number of arts teachers know different skills of microteaching than the Science/Arts student teachers. The overall response data to this item shows that a total of 92.09 per cent respondents responded yes which means most of the student teachers know different skills of microteaching.

By above all interpretations it can be drawn that the student teachers of Karnataka state practice the microteaching skills, so the null minor hypothesis 5 is rejected and the alternative minor hypothesis 5 is accepted.

Null Minor Hypothesis 6

The student teachers of Karnataka state do not practice the microteaching cycle.

F1: *Do you know microteaching cycle?*

F2: *Do you understand different stages of microteaching cycle?*

F3: *Do you feel microteaching cycle wastes much time?*

The data shown in table 4.6 indicates that, for the item F1, 94.29 per cent female and 86.11 per cent male responded yes in gender category, it means more female student teachers know about microteaching cycle than the male. Secondly, for the type of institutions i.e., 100.00 per cent government, 100.00 per cent aided, 87.69 per cent unaided student teachers responded yes, which indicates that all of the government, aided student teachers know about microteaching cycle, which is followed by responses of student teachers from unaided.

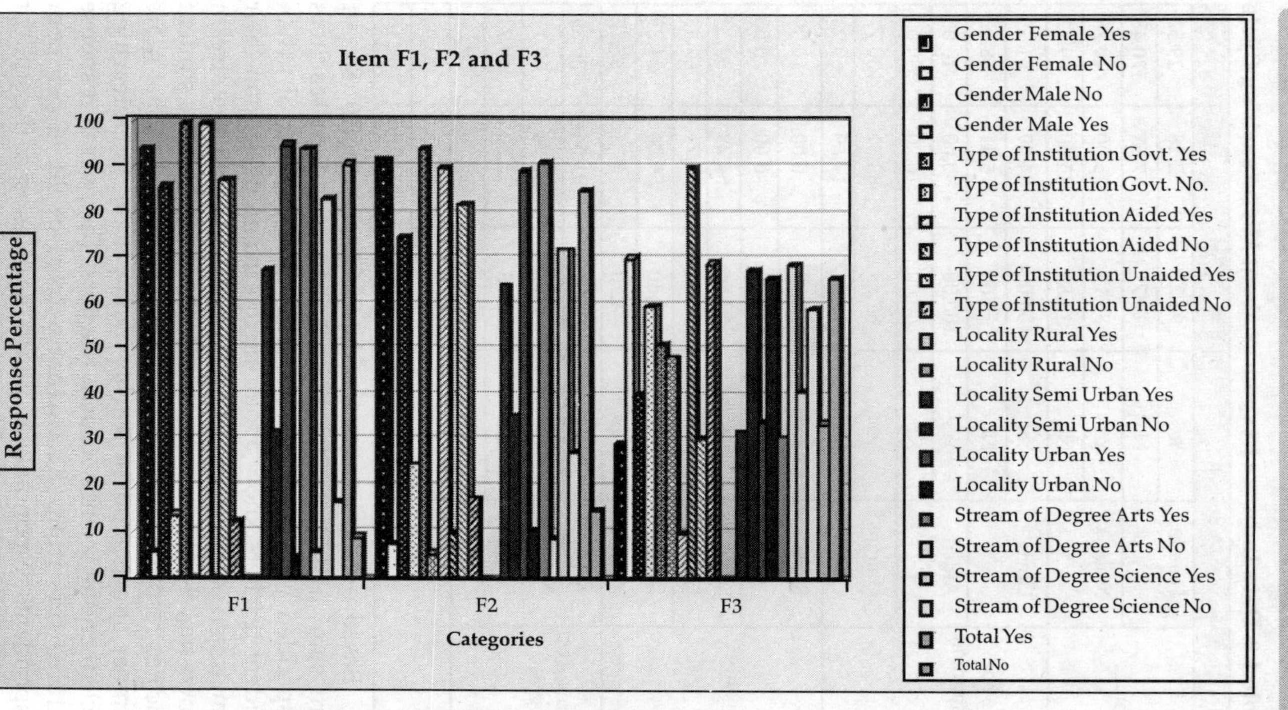

Graph 4.6: **Data Indicate Response about Microteaching Cycle**

Table 4.6: Data Indicate Responses about Microteaching Cycle

Variable		Responses	F1	F2	F3
Gender	Female	Yes	94.29	92.28	29.52
		No	5.71	7.62	70.48
	Male	Yes	86.11	75.00	40.28
		No	13.89	25.00	59.72
Type of Institution	Govt.	Yes	100.00	94.59	51.35
		No	0.00	5.41	48.65
	Aided	Yes	100.00	90.00	10.00
		No	0.00	10.00	90.00
	Unaided	Yes	87.69	82.31	30.77
		No	12.31	17.69	69.23
Locality	Rural	Yes	0.00	0.00	0.00
		No	0.00	0.00	0.00
	Semi-Urban	Yes	67.86	64.29	32.14
		No	32.14	35.71	67.86
	Urban	Yes	95.30	89.26	34.23
		No	4.70	10.74	65.77
Stream of Degree	Arts	Yes	94.31	91.06	30.89
		No	5.69	8.94	69.11
	Science	Yes	83.33	72.22	40.74
		No	16.67	27.78	59.26
Total		Yes	90.96	85.31	33.90
		No	9.04	14.69	66.10

Based on the locality the data indicates that 67.86 per cent semi urban, 95.30 per cent urban student teachers responded yes. This indicates that more number of urban student teachers know about microteaching cycle than their semi urban counterparts. The data based on the degree stream shows that 94.31 per cent arts, 83.33 per cent science student teachers responded yes. It is evident from the data that more number of arts student teachers know about microteaching cycle than the science student teachers. The overall response data to this item shows that a total of 90.96 per cent respondents responded yes, which means most of the student teachers know about microteaching cycle.

For item F2, 92.38 per cent female and 75.00 per cent male responded yes in gender category, it means more female student teachers understand different stages of microteaching cycle than the male. Secondly, for the type of institutions i.e., 94.59 per cent government, 90.00 per cent aided, 82.31 per cent unaided student teachers responded yes, which indicates that most of the government student teachers understand different stages of microteaching cycle, which is followed by responses of student teachers from aided and unaided respectively. Based on the locality the data indicates that 64.29 per cent semi-urban, 89.26 per cent urban student teachers responded yes. This indicates that more number of semi-urban student teachers understand different stages of microteaching cycle than their semi-urban counterparts. The data based on the degree stream shows that 91.06 per cent arts, 72.22 per cent science student teachers responded yes. It is evident from the data that more number of arts student teachers understands different stages of microteaching cycle than the science student teachers. The overall response data to this item shows that a total of 85.31 per cent respondents responded yes, which means most of the student teachers understand different stages of microteaching cycle.

For the item F3, 29.52 per cent female and 40.28 per cent male responded yes in gender category, it means more male student teachers agree that microteaching cycle wastes much time than the female, who appear not to agree with the above statement. Secondly, for the type of institutions i.e., 51.35 per cent government, 10.00 per cent aided, 30.77 per cent unaided student teachers responded yes, which indicates that most of the government institutions student teachers agree that microteaching cycle wastes much time, which is followed by affirmative responses of student teachers from unaided and aided respectively. Based on the locality the data indicates that 32.14 per cent semi-urban, 34.23 per cent urban student teachers responded yes. This indicates that more number of urban student teachers feel that microteaching cycle wastes much time than their semi-urban counterparts. The data based on the degree stream shows that 30.89 per cent arts, 40.74 per cent science student teachers responded yes. It is evident from the data that more number of almost equal proportion of arts and science student teachers feel that microteaching cycle wastes much time, however these responses are less in proportion in comparison to those who do not fee that microteaching cycle wastes much time. The overall response data to this item shows that a total of 33.90 per cent respondents responded yes, which means most of the student teachers do not feel that microteaching cycle wastes much time.

From the above data/interpretations we can draw a conclusion that the student teachers of Karnataka state practice microteaching cycle. Hence, the null minor hypothesis 6 is rejected and the alternative minor hypothesis 6 is accepted.

Null Minor Hypothesis 7

The student teachers of Karnataka state do not know the method of microteaching lesson plan.

G1: *Do your teacher educators verify your microteaching lesson plans?*

G2: *Do you feel any difficulty in preparing microteaching lesson plan?*

G3: *Do you get any special guidance for preparing microteaching lesson plans?*

The data shown in table 4.7 indicates that, for the item G1, 99.05 per cent female and 97.22 per cent male responded yes in gender category, it means that all most all female student teachers agree that their teacher educators verify micro-teaching lesson plans and similar is the feeling of male. Secondly, for the type of institutions i.e., 100.00 per cent government, 100.00 per cent aided, 97.69 per cent unaided student teachers responded yes, which indicates that all of the government, aided student teachers agree that teacher educators verify microteaching lesson plans, which is followed by responses of student teachers from unaided. Based on the locality the data indicates that 92.86 per cent semi-urban, 99.33

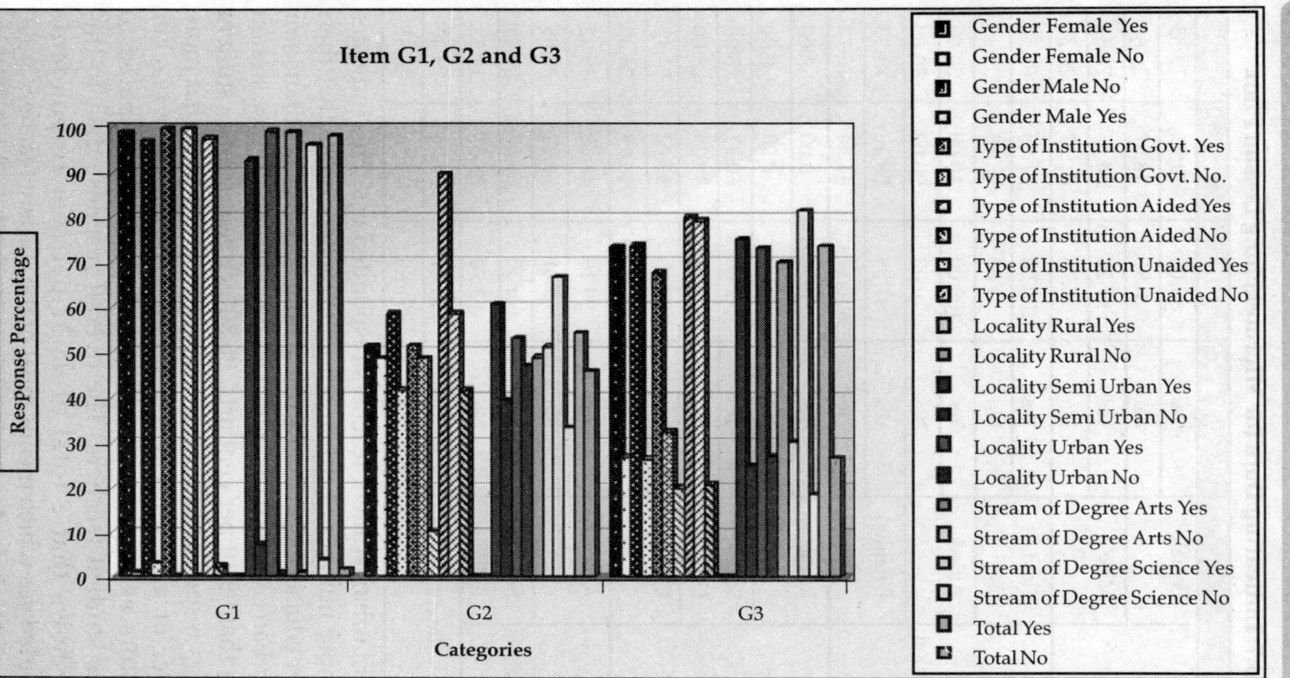

Graph 4.7: **Indicating Data for Microteaching Lesson Plan**

Table 4.7: Indicating Data for Microteaching Lesson Plan

Variable		Responses	G1	G2	G3
Gender	Female	Yes	99.05	51.43	73.33
		No	0.95	48.57	26.67
	Male	Yes	97.22	58.33	73.61
		No	2.78	41.67	26.39
Type of Institution	Govt.	Yes	100.00	51.35	67.57
		No	0.00	48.65	32.43
	Aided	Yes	100.00	10.00	20.00
		No	0.00	90.00	80.00
	Unaided	Yes	97.69	58.46	79.23
		No	2.31	41.54	20.77
Locality	Rural	Yes	0.00	0.00	0.00
		No	0.00	0.00	0.00
	Semi-Urban	Yes	92.86	60.71	75.00
		No	7.14	39.29	25.00
	Urban	Yes	99.33	53.02	73.15
		No	0.67	46.98	26.85
Stream of Degree	Arts	Yes	99.19	48.78	69.92
		No	0.81	51.22	30.08
	Science	Yes	96.30	66.67	81.48
		No	3.70	33.33	18.52
Total		Yes	98.31	54.24	73.45
		No	1.69	45.76	26.55

per cent urban student teachers responded yes. This indicates that more number of urban student teachers agree that their teacher educators verify microteaching lesson plans than their semi urban counterparts. The data based on the degree stream shows that 99.19 per cent arts, 96.30 per cent science student teachers responded yes. It is evident from the data that more number of arts student teachers agree that their teacher educators verify microteaching lesson plans compared to science student teachers. The overall response data to this item shows that a total of 98.31 per cent respondents responded yes which means most of the student teachers agree that their teacher educators verify microteaching lesson plans.

For item G2, 51.43 per cent female and 58.33 per cent male responded yes in gender category, it means more male student teachers feel difficulty in preparing microteaching lesson plan than the female. Secondly, for the type of institutions i.e., 51.35 per cent government, 10.00 per cent aided, 58.46 per cent unaided student teachers responded yes, which indicates that most of the unaided and followed by government institutions student teachers feel difficulty in preparing microteaching lesson plan and the difficulty in writing the lesson plan expressed by the student teachers of aided institutes is quite less. Based on the locality the data indicates that 60.71 per cent semi-urban, 53.02 per cent urban student teachers responded yes. This indicates that more number of semi-urban student teachers feel difficulty in preparing microteaching lesson plan than their urban counterparts. The data based on the degree stream shows that 48.78 per cent arts, 66.67 per cent science student teachers responded yes. It is evident from the data that more number of science student teachers feel difficulty in preparing microteaching lesson plan than the Arts student teachers. The overall response data to this item shows that a total of 54.24 per cent respondents responded yes, which means most of the student teachers feel difficulty in preparing microteaching lesson plan.

For item G3, 73.33 per cent female and 73.61 per cent male responded yes in gender category, it means that both male and female student teachers feel that they get special guidance for preparing microteaching lesson plans. Secondly, for the type of institutions i.e., 67.57 per cent government, 20.00 per cent aided, 79.23 per cent unaided student teachers responded yes, which indicates that most of the unaided, followed by government student teachers feel that they get special guidance for preparing microteaching lesson plans compared to those from unaided institutions. Based on the locality the data indicates that 75.00 per cent semi-urban, 73.15 per cent urban student teachers responded yes. This indicates that more number of semi-urban student teachers feel that they get special guidance for preparing microteaching lesson plans than their urban counterparts. The data based on the degree stream shows that 69.92 per cent arts, 81.48 per cent science student teachers responded yes. It is evident from the data that more number of science student teachers feel that they get special guidance for preparing microteaching lesson plans than the Arts student teachers. The overall response data to this item shows that a total of 73.45 per cent respondents responded yes, which means most of the student teachers feel that they get special guidance for preparing microteaching lesson plans.

From the above data/interpretations we can draw a conclusion that the student teachers of Karnataka state know the method of microteaching lesson plan, so the null minor hypothesis 7 is rejected and the alternative minor hypothesis 7 is accepted.

Null Minor Hypothesis 8

The student teachers of Karnataka state do not involve in organisation of microteaching.

H1: *Do your teacher educators do orientation of microteaching practice?*

H2: *Do your teacher educators present the model microteaching lessons?*

H3: *Do your teacher educators explain different skills of microteaching?*

The data shown in table 4.8 indicates that, for item H1, 96.19 per cent female and 91.67 per cent male responded yes in gender category, it means more female student teachers agree that teacher educators orient for micro teaching practice than the male. Secondly, for the type of institutions i.e., 97.30 per cent government, 90.00 per cent aided, 93.85 per cent unaided student teachers responded yes, which indicates that most of the government student teachers agree that teacher educators orient for microteaching practice, which is followed by responses of student teachers from unaided and aided respectively. Based on the locality the data indicates that 85.71 per cent semi-urban, 95.97 per cent urban student teachers

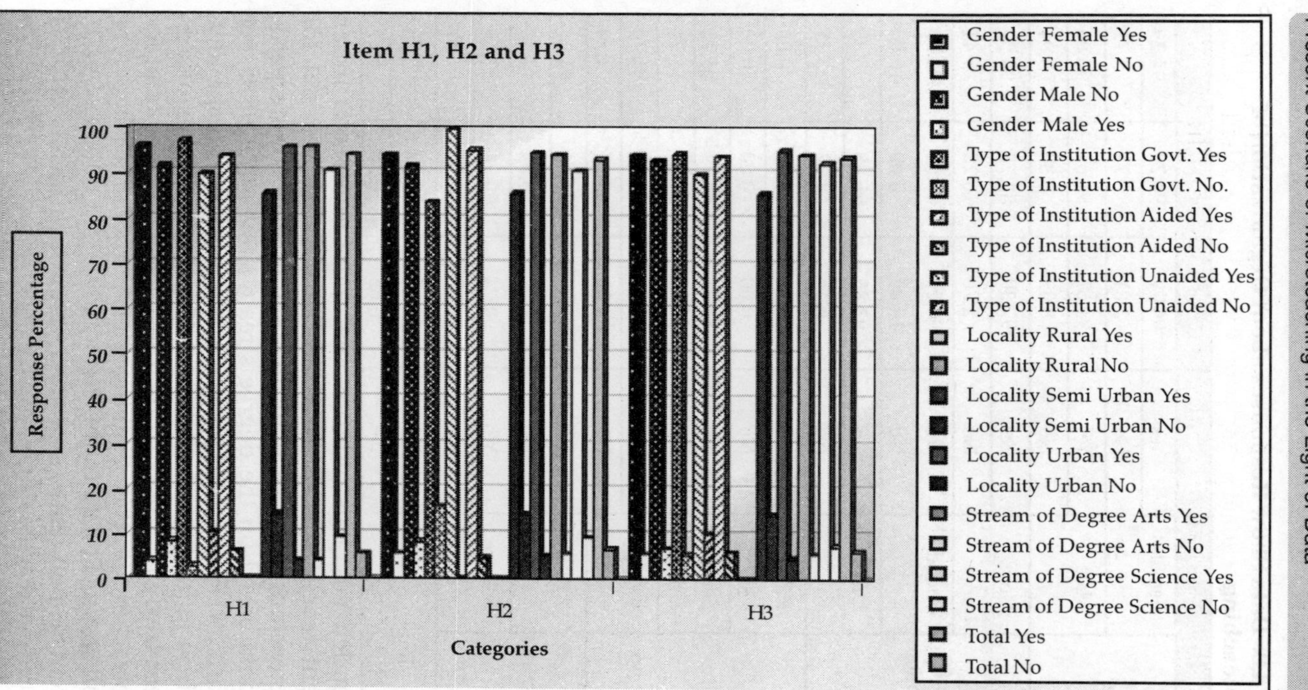

Graph 4.8: **Data Show Response about Organization of Microteaching**

Table 4.8: Data Show Responses about Organization of Microteaching

Variable		Responses	H1	H2	H3
Gender	Female	Yes	96.19	94.29	94.29
		No	3.81	5.71	5.71
	Male	Yes	91.67	91.67	93.06
		No	8.33	8.33	6.94
Type of Institution	Govt.	Yes	97.30	83.78	94.59
		No	2.70	16.22	5.41
	Aided	Yes	90.00	100.00	90.00
		No	10.00	0.00	10.00
	Unaided	Yes	93.85	95.38	93.85
		No	6.15	4.62	6.15
Locality	Rural	Yes	0.00	0.00	0.00
		No	0.00	0.00	0.00
	Semi-Urban	Yes	85.71	85.71	85.71
		No	14.29	14.29	14.29
	Urban	Yes	95.97	94.63	95.30
		No	4.03	5.37	4.70
Stream of Degree	Arts	Yes	95.93	94.31	94.31
		No	4.07	5.69	5.69
	Science	Yes	90.74	90.74	92.59
		No	9.26	9.26	7.41
Total		Yes	94.35	93.22	93.79
		No	5.65	6.78	6.21

responded yes. This indicates that more number of urban student teachers agree that teacher educators orient for microteaching practice than their semi-urban counterparts. The data based on the degree stream shows that 95.93 per cent arts, 90.74 per cent science student teachers responded yes. It is evident from the data that more number of arts student teachers agree that their teacher educators orient for microteaching practice than the science student teachers. The overall response data to this item shows that a total of 94.35 per cent respondents responded yes, which means most of the student teachers agree that teacher educators orient for microteaching practice.

For item H2, 94.29 per cent female and 91.67 per cent male responded yes in gender category, it means more female student teachers agree that their teacher educators present the model microteaching lessons than the male. Secondly, for the type of institutions i.e., 83.78 per cent government, 100.00 per cent aided, 95.38 per cent unaided student teachers responded yes, which indicates that all of the aided student teachers agree that their teacher educators present the model microteaching lessons, which is followed by responses of student teachers from unaided and government respectively. Based on the locality the data indicates that 85.71 per cent semi-urban, 94.63 per cent urban student teachers responded yes. This indicates that more number of urban student teachers agree that their teacher educators present the model micro-teaching lessons than their semi-urban counterparts. The data based on the degree stream shows that 94.31 per cent arts, 90.74 per cent science student teachers responded yes. It is evident from the data that more number of arts student teachers agree that their teacher educators present the model microteaching lessons than the science student teachers. The overall response data to this item shows that a total of 93.22 per cent respondents responded yes, which means most of the student teachers agree that their teacher educators present the model microteaching lessons.

For item H3, 94.29 per cent female and 93.06 per cent male responded yes in gender category and it means more female student teachers agree that their teacher educators explain different skills of microteaching than the male/female. Secondly, for the type of institutions i.e., 94.59 per cent government, 90.00 per cent aided, 93.85 per cent unaided student teachers responded yes, which indicates that most of the government student teachers agree that their teacher educators explain different skills of microteaching, which is followed by responses of student teachers from unaided and aided respectively. Based on the locality the data indicates that 85.71 per cent semi-urban, 95.30 per cent urban student teachers responded yes. This indicates that more number of urban student teachers agree that their teacher educators explain different skills of microteaching than their semi-urban counterparts. The data based on the degree stream shows that 94.31 per cent arts, 92.59 per cent science student teachers responded yes. It is evident from the data that more number of arts student teachers agree that their teacher educators explain different skills of microteaching than the science student teachers. The overall response data to this item shows that a total of 93.79 per cent respondents responded yes, which means most of the student teachers agree that their teacher educators explain different skills of microteaching.

From the above data/interpretations we can draw a conclusion that the student teachers of Karnataka state get involved in organisation of microteaching, so the null minor hypothesis 8 is rejected and the alternative minor hypothesis 8 is accepted.

Null Minor Hypothesis 9

The student teachers of Karnataka state do not observe the microteaching lesson plans by using observation schedule.

I-1: *Do you observe the microteaching lessons of your peer groups?*

I-2: *Do you know how to observe the microteaching lessons?*

I-3: *Did your teacher educators give different observation schedule for observation of different microteaching skills?*

The data shown in table 4.9 indicates that, for item I-1, 98.10 per cent female and 94.44 per cent male responded yes in gender category, it means more female student teachers agree that they observe microteaching lessons of their peer groups than the male. Secondly, for the type of institutions i.e., 100.00 per cent government, 100.00 per cent aided, 95.38 per cent unaided student teachers responded yes, which indicates that all of the government and aided student teachers agree that they observe microteaching lessons of their peer groups, which is followed by responses of student teachers from unaided.

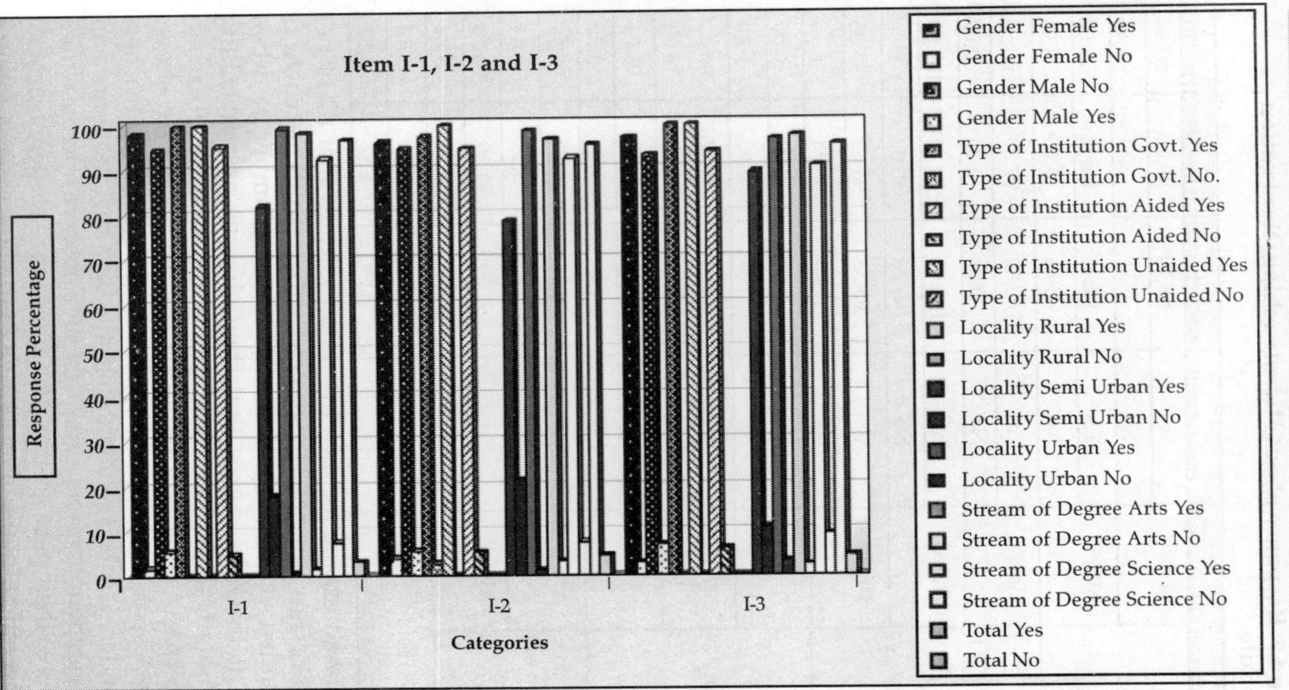

Graph 4.9: **Responses about Microteaching Observation Schedule**

Table 4.9: Response about Microteaching Observation Schedule

Variable		Responses	I-1	I-2	I-3
Gender	Female	Yes	98.10	96.19	97.14
		No	1.90	3.81	2.86
	Male	Yes	94.44	94.44	93.06
		No	5.56	5.56	6.94
Type of Institution	Govt.	Yes	100.00	97.30	100.00
		No	0.00	2.70	0.00
	Aided	Yes	100.00	100.00	100.00
		No	0.00	0.00	0.00
	Unaided	Yes	95.38	94.62	93.85
		No	4.62	5.38	6.15
Locality	Rural	Yes	0.00	0.00	0.00
		No	0.00	0.00	0.00
	Semi-Urban	Yes	82.14	78.57	89.29
		No	17.86	21.43	10.71
	Urban	Yes	99.33	98.66	96.64
		No	0.67	1.34	3.36
Stream of Degree	Arts	Yes	98.37	96.75	97.56
		No	1.63	3.25	2.44
	Science	Yes	92.59	92.59	90.74
		No	7.41	7.14	9.26
Total		Yes	96.61	95.48	95.48
		No	3.39	4.52	4.52

Based on the locality the data indicates that 82.14 per cent semi-urban, 99.33 per cent urban student teachers responded yes. This indicates that more number of urban student teachers agree that they observe microteaching lessons of their peer groups than their semi-urban counterparts. The data based on the degree stream shows that 98.37 per cent arts, 92.59 per cent science student teachers responded yes. It is evident from the data that more number of arts student teachers agree that they observe microteaching lessons of their peer groups than the science student teachers. The overall response data to this item shows that a total of

96.61 per cent respondents responded yes, which means most of the student teachers agree that they observe microteaching lessons of their peer groups.

For item I-2, 96.19 per cent female and 94.44 per cent male responded yes in gender category, it means more female student teachers agree that they know how to observe the microteaching lessons than the male. Secondly, for the type of institutions i.e., 97.30 per cent government, 100.00 per cent aided, 94.62 per cent unaided student teachers responded yes, which indicates that all of the aided student teachers agree that they know how to observe the micro-teaching lessons, which is followed by responses of student teachers from government and unaided respectively. Based on the locality the data indicates that 78.57 per cent semi-urban, 98.66 per cent urban student teachers responded yes. This indicates that more number of urban student teachers agree that they know how to observe the microteaching lessons than their semi-urban counterparts. The data based on the degree stream shows that 96.75 per cent arts, 92.59 per cent science student teachers responded yes. It is evident from the data that more number of arts student teachers agree that they know how to observe the microteaching lessons than the science student teachers. The overall response data to this item shows that a total of 95.48 per cent respondents responded yes, which means most of the student teachers agree that they know how to observe the microteaching lessons.

For item I-3, 97.14 per cent female and 93.06 per cent male responded yes in gender category, it means more female student teachers agree that their teacher educators gave different observation schedule for observation of different microteaching skills than the male. Secondly, for the type of institutions i.e., 100.00 per cent government, 100.00 per cent aided, 93.85 per cent unaided student teachers responded yes, which indicates that all of the government and aided student teachers agree that their teacher educators gave different observation schedule for observation of different microteaching skills, which is followed by responses of student teachers from unaided. Based on the locality the data indicates that 89.29 per cent semi-urban, 96.64 per cent urban student teachers responded yes. This indicates that more number of urban student teachers agree that their teacher educators gave different observation schedule for observation of different microteaching skills than their semi-urban counterparts. The data based on the degree stream shows that 97.56 per cent arts, 90.74 per cent science student teachers responded yes. It is evident from the data that more number of arts student teachers agree that their teacher educators gave different observation schedule for observation of different microteaching skills than the science student teachers. The overall response data to this item shows that a total of 95.48 per cent respondents responded yes which means most of the student teachers agree that their teacher educators gave different observation schedule for observation of different microteaching skills.

From the above data/interpretations we can draw a conclusion that the student teachers of Karnataka state observe the microteaching lesson plans by using observation schedule, so the null minor hypothesis 9 is rejected and the alternative minor hypothesis 9 is accepted.

Null Minor Hypothesis 10

The student teachers of Karnataka state do not know the planning of microteaching.

J1: *Do you know the planning of microteaching?*

J2: *Do you get sufficient planning time for microteaching?*

J3: *Do you know different components which come under planning of microteaching?*

The data shown in table 4.10 indicates that, for the item J1, 96.19 per cent female and 87.50 per cent male responded yes in gender category, it means more female student teachers agree that they know the planning of microteaching than the male. Secondly, for the type of institutions i.e., 100.00 per cent government, 90.00 per cent aided, 90.77 per cent unaided

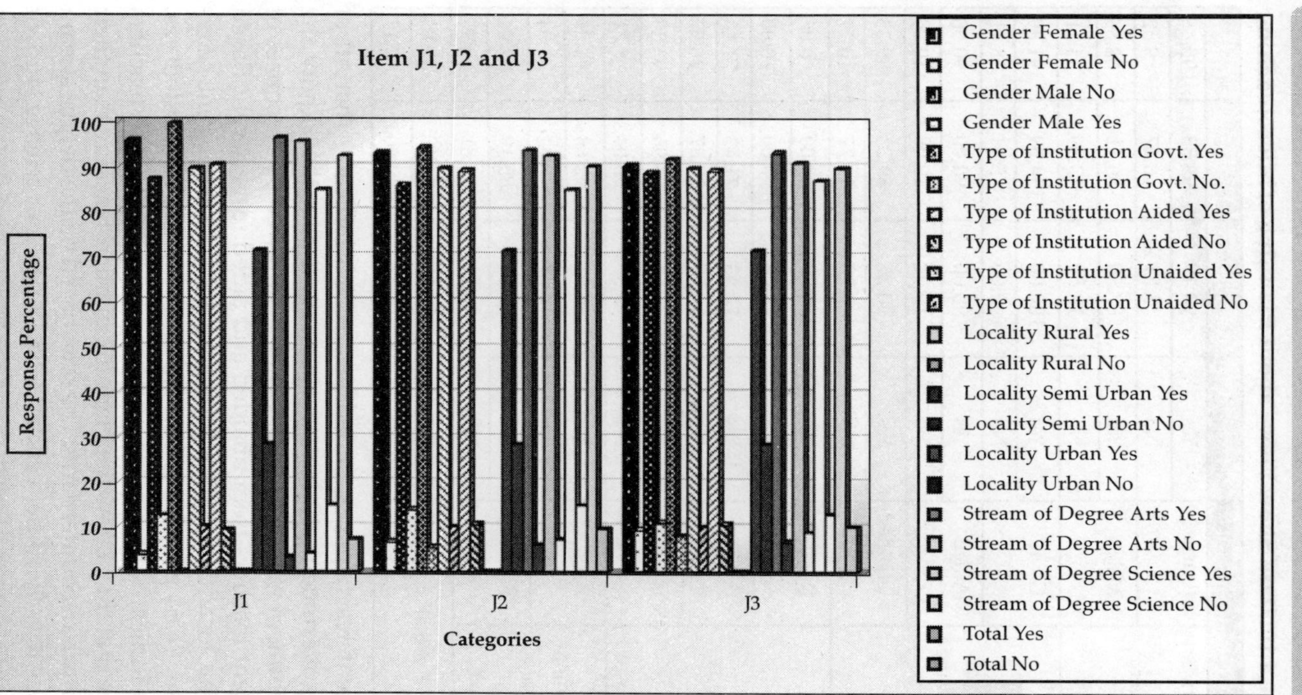

Graph 4.10: **Data Show Views about Planning of Microteaching**

Table 4.10: Data Show Views about Planning of Microteaching

Variable		Responses	J1	J2	J3
Gender	Female	Yes	96.19	93.33	90.48
		No	3.81	6.67	9.52
	Male	Yes	87.50	86.11	88.89
		No	12.50	13.89	11.11
Type of Institution	Govt.	Yes	100.00	94.59	91.89
		No	0.00	5.41	8.11
	Aided	Yes	90.00	90.00	90.00
		No	10.00	10.00	10.00
	Unaided	Yes	90.77	89.23	89.23
		No	9.23	10.77	10.77
Locality	Rural	Yes	0.00	0.00	0.00
		No	0.00	0.00	0.00
	Semi-Urban	Yes	71.43	71.43	71.43
		No	28.57	28.57	28.57
	Urban	Yes	96.64	93.96	93.29
		No	3.36	6.04	6.71
Stream of Degree	Arts	Yes	95.93	92.68	91.06
		No	4.07	7.32	8.94
	Science	Yes	85.19	85.19	87.04
		No	14.81	14.81	12.96
Total		Yes	92.66	90.40	89.83
		No	7.34	9.60	10.17

student teachers responded yes, which indicates that all of the government student teachers agree that they know the planning of microteaching, which is followed by responses of student teachers from unaided and aided respectively. Based on the locality the data indicates that 71.43 per cent semi-urban, 96.64 per cent urban student teachers responded yes. This indicates that more number of urban student teachers agree that they know the planning of microteaching than their semi-urban counterparts. The data based on the degree stream shows that 95.93 per cent arts, 85.19 per cent science student teachers responded yes. It is evident from the data that more number of arts student teachers agree that they know the planning of microteaching than the science student teachers. The overall response data to this item shows that a total of 92.66 per cent respondents responded yes, which means most of the student teachers agree that they know the planning of microteaching.

For item J2, 93.33 per cent female and 86.11 per cent male responded yes in gender category, it means more female student teachers agree that they get sufficient planning time for microteaching than the male. Secondly, for the type of institutions i.e., 94.59 per cent government, 90.00 per cent aided, 89.23 per cent unaided student teachers responded yes, which indicates that most of the government student teachers agree that they get sufficient planning time for microteaching, which is followed by responses of student teachers from aided and unaided respectively.

Based on the locality the data indicates that 71.43 per cent semi-urban, 93.96 per cent urban student teachers responded yes. This indicates that more number of urban student teachers agree that they get sufficient planning time for microteaching than their semi-urban counterparts. The data based on the degree stream shows that 92.68 per cent arts, 85.19 per cent science student teachers responded yes. It is evident from the data that more number of arts student teachers agree that they get sufficient planning time for microteaching than the science student teachers. The overall response data to this item shows that a total of 90.40 per cent respondents responded yes, which means most of the student teachers agree that they get sufficient planning time for microteaching.

For item J3, 90.48 per cent female and 88.89 per cent male responded yes in gender category, it means more female student teachers agree that they know different components which come under planning of microteaching than the male. Secondly, for the type of institutions i.e., 91.89 per cent government, 90.00 per cent aided, 89.23 per cent unaided student teachers responded yes, which indicates that most of the government student teachers agree that they know different components which come under planning of microteaching, which is followed by responses of student teachers from aided and unaided respectively. Based on the locality the data indicates that 71.43 per cent semi-urban, 93.29 per cent urban student teachers responded yes. This indicates that more number of urban student teachers agree that they know different components which come under planning of microteaching than their semi-urban counterparts. The data based on the degree stream shows that 91.06 per cent arts, 87.04 per cent science student teachers responded yes. It is evident from the data that more number of arts student teachers agree that they know different components which come under planning of microteaching than the science student teachers. The overall response data to this item shows that a total of 89.83 per cent respondents responded yes, which means most of the student teachers agree that they know different components which come under planning of microteaching.

From the above data/interpretations we can draw a conclusion that the student teachers of Karnataka state agree that they know the planning of microteaching, so the null minor hypothesis 10 is rejected and the alternative minor hypothesis 10 is accepted.

Null Minor Hypothesis 11

The student teachers of Karnataka state do not know the importance of feedback.

K1: *Do you know the importance of Feedback?*

K2: *Do you feel giving feedback is helpful in improving the skills?*

K3: *Do you agree with the statement: "Audio-Video feedback is superior in microteaching than the only oral feedback of teacher educators and student-teachers"?*

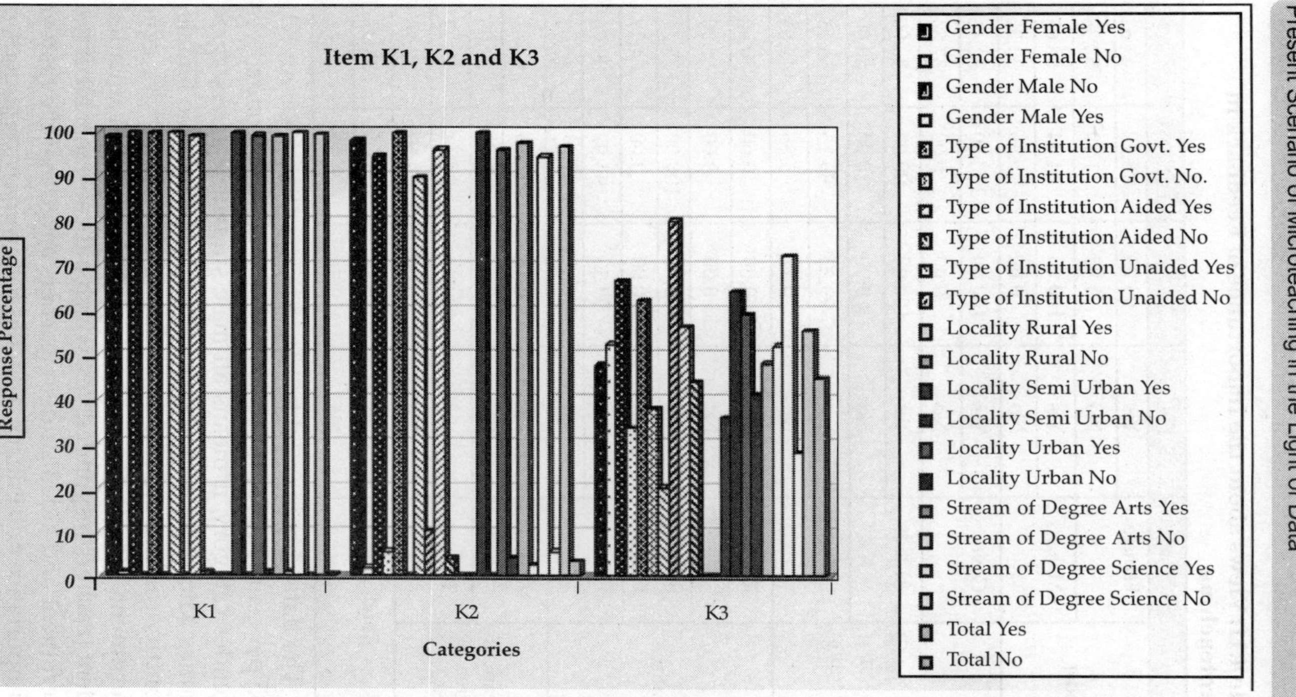

Graph 4.11: **Views about the Importance of Feedback in Microteaching**

Table 4.11: Views about the Importance of Feedback in Microteaching

Variable		Responses	K1	K2	K3
Gender	Female	Yes	99.05	98.10	47.62
		No	0.95	1.90	52.38
	Male	Yes	100.00	94.44	66.67
		No	0.00	5.56	33.33
Type of Institution	Govt.	Yes	100.00	100.00	62.16
		No	0.00	0.00	37.84
	Aided	Yes	100.00	90.00	20.00
		No	0.00	10.00	80.00
	Unaided	Yes	99.23	96.15	56.15
		No	0.77	3.85	43.85
Locality	Rural	Yes	0.00	0.00	0.00
		No	0.00	0.00	0.00
	Semi-Urban	Yes	100.00	100.00	35.71
		No	0.00	0.00	64.29
	Urban	Yes	99.33	95.97	59.06
		No	0.67	4.03	40.94
Stream of Degree	Arts	Yes	99.19	97.56	47.97
		No	0.81	2.44	52.03
	Science	Yes	100.00	94.44	72.22
		No	0.00	5.56	27.78
Total		Yes	99.44	96.61	55.37
		No	0.56	3.39	44.63

The data shown in table 4.11 indicates that, for item K1, 99.05 per cent female and 100.00 per cent male responded yes in gender category, it means all male student teachers agree that they know the importance of feedback than the female. Secondly, for the type of institutions i.e., 100.00 per cent government, 100.00 per cent aided, 99.23 per cent unaided student teachers responded yes, which indicates that all of the government and aided student teachers agree that they know the importance of feedback, which is followed by responses of student teachers from unaided. Based on the locality the data indicates that 100.00 per cent semi-urban, 99.33 per cent urban student teachers responded yes. This indicates that all of semi-urban student teachers agree that they know the importance of feedback than their urban counterparts. The data based on the degree stream shows that 99.19 per cent arts, 100.00 per cent science student teachers responded yes. It is evident from the data that all the science student teachers agree that they know the importance of feedback than the Arts student teachers. The overall response data to this item shows that a total of 99.44 per cent respondents responded yes, which means most of the student teachers agree that they know the importance of feedback.

For item K2, 98.10 per cent female and 94.44 per cent male responded yes in gender category and it means more female student teachers feel that giving feedback is helpful in improving the skills than the male. Secondly, for the type of institutions i.e., 100.00 per cent government, 90.00 per cent aided, 96.15 per cent unaided student teachers responded yes, which indicates that all of the government student teachers feel that giving feedback is helpful in improving the skills, which is followed by responses of student teachers from unaided and aided respectively. Based on the locality the data indicates that 100.00 per cent semi-urban, 95.97 per cent urban student teachers responded yes. This indicates that all the semi-urban student teachers feel that giving feedback is helpful in improving the skills than their urban counterparts. The data based on the degree stream shows that 97.56 per cent arts, 94.44 per cent science student teachers responded yes. It is evident from the data that more number of arts student teachers feel that giving feedback is helpful in improving the skills than the science student teachers. The overall response data to this item shows that a total of 96.61 per cent respondents responded yes, which means most of the student teachers feel that giving feedback is helpful in improving the skills.

For item K3, 47.62 per cent female and 66.67 per cent male responded yes in gender category, it means more male student teachers agree that audio-vide feedback is superior to oral feedback than the female. Secondly, for the type of institutions i.e., 62.16 per cent government, 20.00 per cent aided, 56.15 per cent unaided student teachers responded yes, which indicates that most of the government student teachers agree that audio-vide feedback is superior to oral feedback, which is followed by responses of student teachers from unaided and aided respectively. Based on the locality the data indicates that 35.71 per cent semi-urban, 59.06 per cent urban student teachers responded yes. This indicates that more number of urban student teachers agree that audio-vide feedback is superior to oral feedback than their semi-urban counterparts. The data based on the degree stream shows that 47.97 per cent arts, 72.22 per cent science student teachers responded yes. It is evident from the data that more number of science student teachers agree that audio-vide feedback is superior to oral feedback than the science/arts student teachers. The overall response data to this item shows that a total of 55.37 per cent respondents responded yes which means most of the student teachers agree that audio-vide feedback is superior to oral feedback.

From the above data/interpretations we can draw a conclusion that the student teachers of Karnataka state agree that they know the importance of feedback, so the null minor hypothesis 11 is rejected and the alternative minor hypothesis 11 is accepted.

Null Minor Hypothesis 12

The student teachers of Karnataka state do not get the demonstration of microteaching skills.

L1: *Do you think that before practicing the skills demonstration has to be given?*

L2: *Did your teacher educators give you sufficient demonstrations in microteaching skills?*

L3: *Do you think demonstrations should be given to maximum number of skills?*

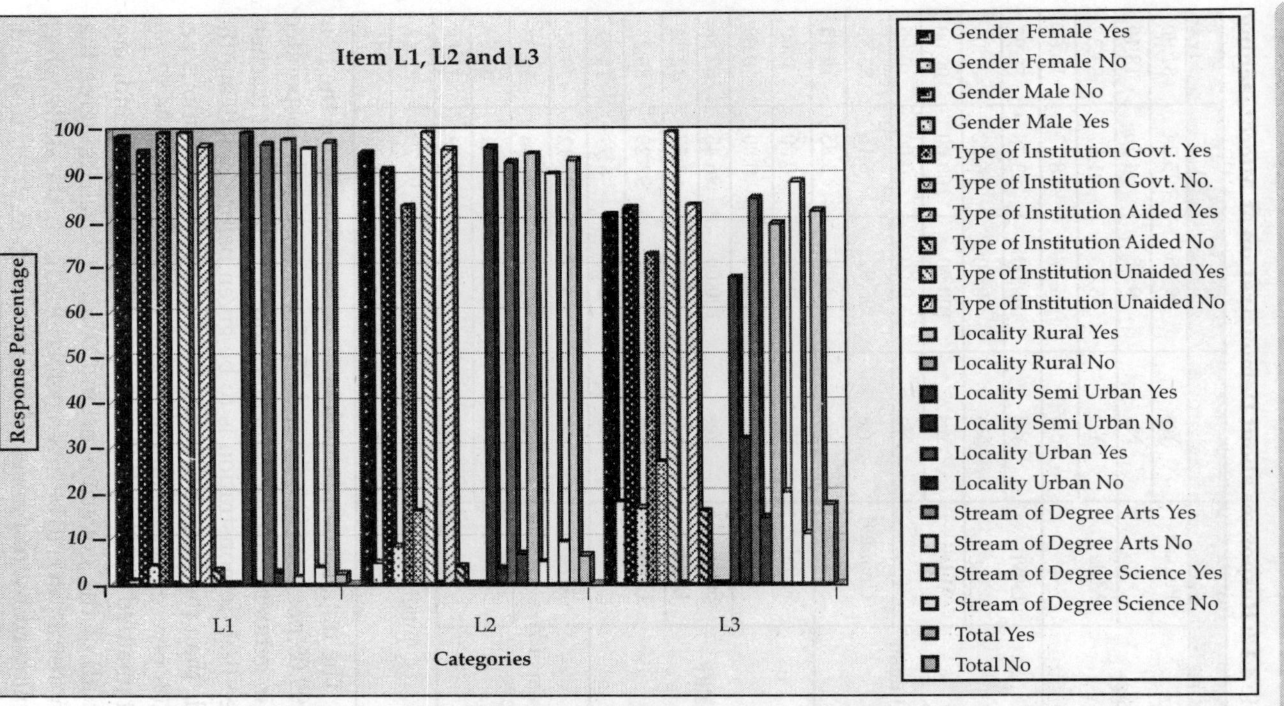

Graph 4.12: **Responses about Demonstration of Microteaching**

Table 4.12: Responses about Demonstration of Microteaching

Variable		Responses	L1	L2	L3
Gender	Female	Yes	99.05	95.24	81.90
		No	0.95	4.76	18.10
	Male	Yes	95.83	91.67	83.33
		No	4.17	8.33	16.67
Type of Institution	Govt.	Yes	100.00	83.78	72.97
		No	0.00	16.22	27.03
	Aided	Yes	100.00	100.00	100.00
		No	0.00	0.00	0.00
	Unaided	Yes	96.92	96.15	83.85
		No	3.08	3.85	16.15
Locality	Rural	Yes	0.00	0.00	0.00
		No	0.00	0.00	0.00
	Semi Urban	Yes	100.00	96.43	67.86
		No	0.00	3.57	32.14
	Urban	Yes	97.32	93.29	85.23
		No	2.68	6.71	14.77
Stream of Degree	Arts	Yes	98.37	95.12	79.67
		No	1.63	4.88	20.33
	Science	Yes	96.30	90.74	88.89
		No	3.70	9.26	11.11
Total		Yes	97.74	93.79	82.49
		No	2.26	6.21	17.51

The data shown in table 4.12 indicates that, for the item L1, 99.05 per cent female and 95.83 per cent male responded yes in gender category, it means more female student teachers agree that demonstration is to be given before practicing the skills than the male. Secondly, for the type of institutions i.e., 100.00 per cent government, 100.00 per cent aided, 96.92 per cent unaided student teachers responded yes, which indicates that all of the government and student teachers agree that demonstration is to be given before practicing the skills, which is followed by responses of student teachers from unaided.

Based on the locality the data indicates that 100.00 per cent semi-urban, 97.32 per cent urban student teachers responded yes. This indicates that all the semi-urban student teachers agree that demonstration is to be given before practicing the skills than their urban counterparts. The data based on the degree stream shows that 98.37 per cent arts, 96.30 per cent science student teachers responded yes. It is evident from the data that more number of arts student teachers agree that demonstration is to be given before practicing the skills than the science student teachers. The overall response data to this item shows that a total of 97.74 per cent respondents responded yes, which means most of the student teachers agree that demonstration is to be given before practicing the skills.

For item L2, 95.24 per cent female and 91.67 per cent male responded yes in gender category, it means more female student teachers agree that the teacher educators gave sufficient demonstrations in microteaching skills than the male. Secondly, for the type of institutions i.e., 83.78 per cent government, 100.00 per cent aided, 96.15 per cent unaided student teachers responded yes, which indicates that all of the aided student teachers agree that the teacher educators gave sufficient demonstrations in microteaching skills, which is followed by responses of student teachers from unaided and government respectively. Based on the locality the data indicates that 96.43 per cent semi-urban, 93.29 per cent urban student teachers responded yes. This indicates that more number of semi-urban student teachers agree that the teacher educators gave sufficient demonstrations in microteaching skills than their urban counterparts. The data based on the degree stream shows that 95.12 per cent arts, 90.74 per cent science student teachers responded yes. It is evident from the data that more number of arts student teachers agree that the teacher educators gave sufficient demonstrations in microteaching skills than the science student teachers. The overall response data to this item shows that a total of 93.79 per cent respondents responded yes, which means most of the student teachers agree that the teacher educators gave sufficient demonstrations in microteaching skills.

For item L3, 81.90 per cent female and 83.33 per cent male responded yes in gender, it means more male student teachers agree that demonstration should be given to maximum number of skills than the female. Secondly, for the type of institutions i.e., 72.97 per cent government, 100.00 per cent aided, 83.85 per cent unaided student teachers responded yes, which indicates that all of the aided student teachers agree that demonstration should be given to maximum number of skills, which is followed by responses of student teachers from unaided and government respectively. Based on the locality the data indicates that 67.86 per cent semi-urban, 85.23 per cent urban student teachers responded yes. This indicates that more number of urban student teachers agree that demonstration should be given to maximum number of skills than their semi-urban counterparts. The data based on the degree stream shows that 79.67 per cent arts, 88.89 per cent science student teachers responded yes. It is evident from the data that more number of science student teachers agree that demonstration should be given to maximum number of skills than the arts student teachers. The overall response data to this item shows that a total of 82.49 per cent respondents responded yes, which means most of the student teachers agree that demonstration should be given to maximum number of skills.

From the above data/interpretations we can draw a conclusion that the student teachers of Karnataka state agree that they get sufficient demonstration of microteaching skills, so the null minor hypothesis 12 is rejected and the alternative minor hypothesis 12 is accepted.

ITEMWISE PERCENTAGE ANALYSIS FOR OPINIONNAIRE

Null Minor Hypothesis 13

The teacher educators of Karnataka state do not think that microteaching cycle should be introduced compulsorily to the student-teachers of B.Ed. course.

O1: *Do you think that microteaching cycle should be introduced compulsorily to the student-teachers of B.Ed. course?*

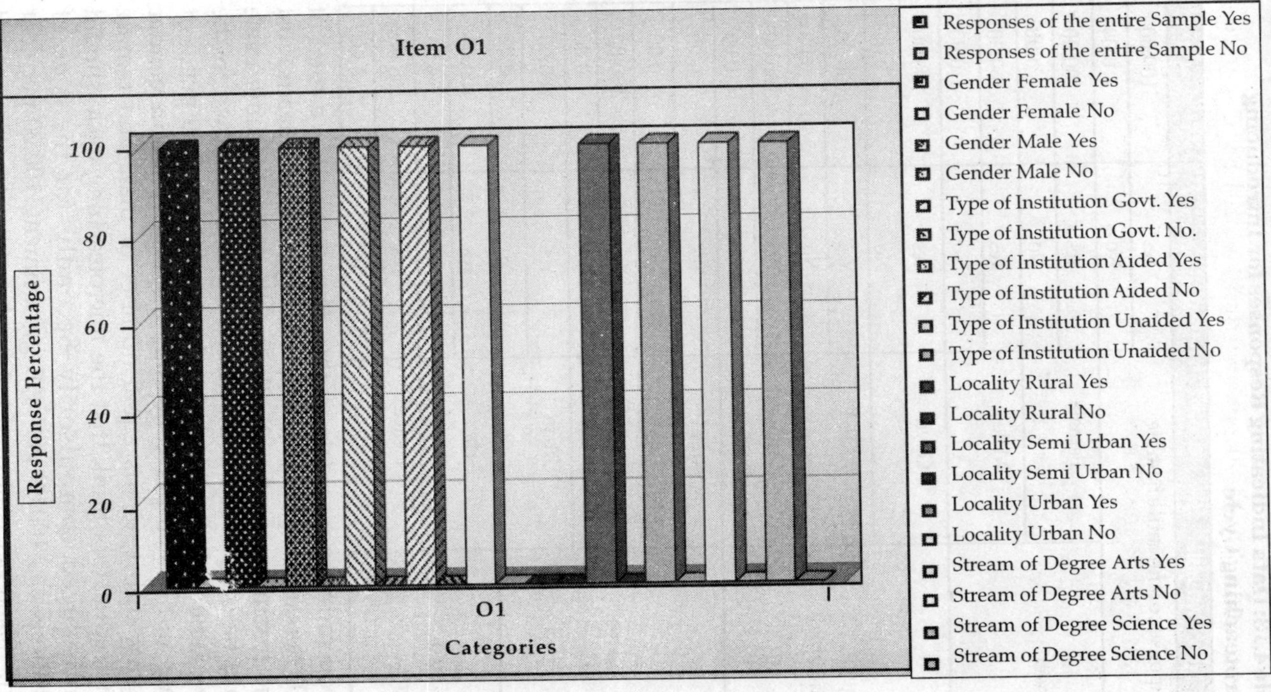

Graph 4.13: **Responses about Introducing Microteaching Cycle**

Table 4.13: Data Indicating Responses for Introducing Microteaching Cycle

Variable		Responses	O1
Responses of the entire Sample		Yes	100.00
		No	0.00
Gender	Female	Yes	100.00
		No	0.00
	Male	Yes	100.00
		No	0.00
Type of Institution	Govt.	Yes	100.00
		No	0.00
	Aided	Yes	100.00
		No	0.00
	Unaided	Yes	100.00
		No	0.00
Locality	Rural	Yes	0.00
		No	0.00
	Semi-Urban	Yes	100.00
		No	0.00
	Urban	Yes	100.00
		No	0.00
Stream of Degree	Arts	Yes	100.00
		No	0.00
	Science	Yes	100.00
		No	0.00

The overall response data to this item shows that a total of 100.00 per cent respondents responded yes, which means most of the teacher educators think that the microteaching cycle should be introduced compulsorily. The data shown in the above table indicates that, for the item O1, 100.00 per cent female and 100.00 per cent male responded yes in gender category and it means equal number of male and female teacher educators think that the microteaching cycle should be introduced compulsorily. Secondly, for the type of institutions i.e., 100.00 per cent government, 100.00 per cent aided, 100.00 per cent unaided teacher educators responded yes, which indicates that all of the government, aided and unaided teacher educators think that the microteaching cycle should be introduced compulsorily. Based on the locality the data indicates that 100.00 per cent semi-urban, 100.00 per cent urban teacher educators responded yes. This indicates that equal number of urban and semi-urban student teachers think that the microteaching cycle should be introduced compulsorily. The data based on the degree stream shows that 100.00 per cent arts, 100.00 per cent science teacher educators responded yes. It is evident from the data that equal number of arts and science teacher educators think that the microteaching cycle should be introduced compulsorily.

From the above mentioned data and interpretations we can draw a conclusion that the teacher educators of Karnataka state think that the microteaching cycle should be introduced compulsorily, so the null minor hypothesis 13 is rejected and the alternative minor hypothesis 13 is accepted.

Null Minor Hypothesis 14

The teacher educators of Karnataka state do not feel it is necessary for teacher educators of B.Ed. to demonstrate all the skills of microteaching.

O2: *Do you feel it is necessary for teacher educators of B.Ed to demonstrate all the skills of microteaching?*

The data shown in table 4.14 indicates that, for the item O2, 100.00 per cent female and 100.00 per cent male responded yes in gender category, it means both male and female teacher educators agree that they demonstrate skills of microteaching. Secondly, for the type of institutions i.e., 100.00 per cent government, 100.00 per cent aided, 100.00 per cent unaided teacher educators responded yes, which indicates that all of the government, aided and unaided teacher educators agree that they demonstrate skills of microteaching. Based on the locality the data indicates that 100.00 per cent semi-urban, 100.00 per cent urban teacher educators responded yes. This indicates that all the teacher educators agree that they demonstrate skills of microteaching. The data based on the degree stream shows that 100.00 per cent arts, 100.00 per cent science teacher educators responded yes. It is evident from the data that more number of arts/science teacher educators agree that they demonstrate skills of microteaching. The overall response data to this item shows that a total of 100.00 per cent respondents responded yes, which means most of the teacher educators agree that they demonstrate skills of microteaching.

From the above mentioned data and interpretations we can draw a conclusion that the teacher educators of Karnataka state agree that it is necessary to demonstrate skills of microteaching, so the null minor hypothesis 14 is rejected and the alternative minor hypothesis 14 is accepted.

Table 4.14: Responses about Demonstrating of Skills in Microteaching

Variable		Responses	O2
Responses of the entire Sample		Yes	100.00
		No	0.00
Gender	Female	Yes	100.00
		No	0.00
	Male	Yes	100.00
		No	0.00
Type of Institution	Govt.	Yes	100.00
		No	0.00
	Aided	Yes	100.00
		No	0.00
	Unaided	Yes	100.00
		No	0.00
Locality	Rural	Yes	0.00
		No	0.00
	Semi-Urban	Yes	100.00
		No	0.00
	Urban	Yes	100.00
		No	0.00
Stream of Degree	Arts	Yes	100.00
		No	0.00
	Science	Yes	100.00
		No	0.00

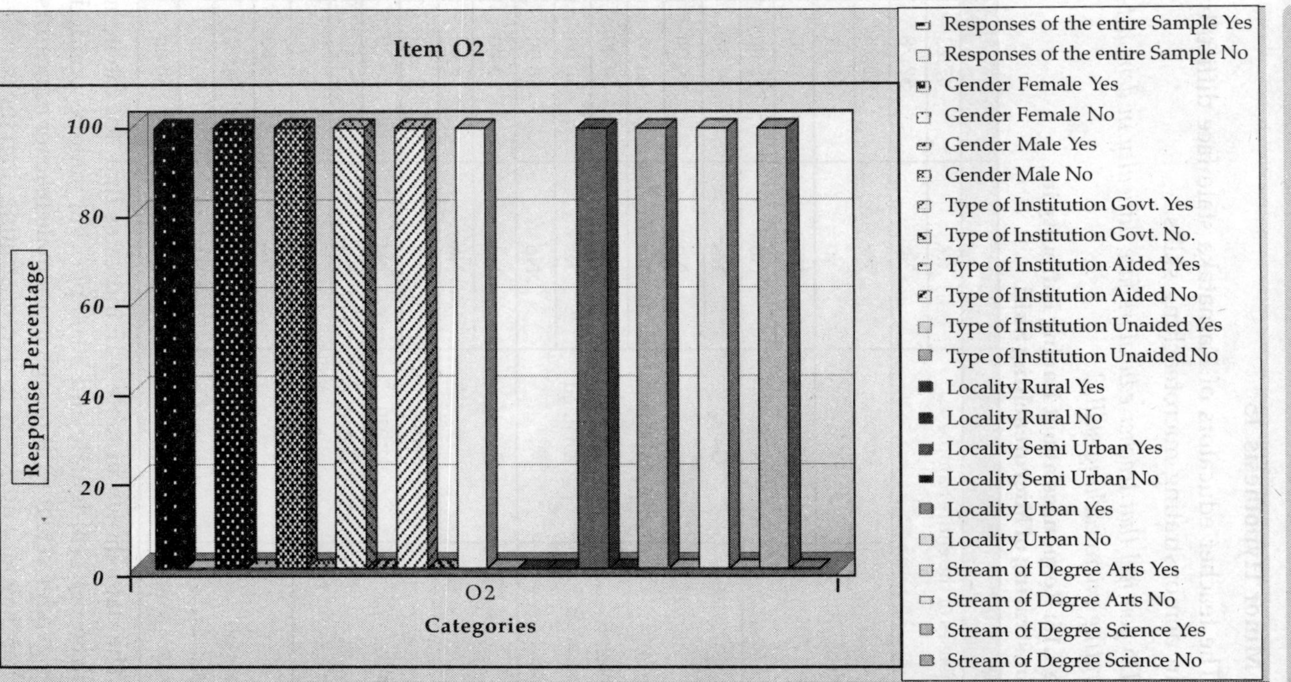

Graph 4.14: **Responses about Demonstrating of Skill in Microteaching**

Null Minor Hypothesis 15

The teacher educators of Karnataka state face difficulty in demonstrating microteaching skills.

O3: *Do you feel that teacher educators face difficulty in demonstrating microteaching skills?*

Table 4.15: Responses about Facing Diffculty in Demonstrating of Microteaching Skill

Variable		Responses	O3
Responses of the entire Sample		Yes	47.22
		No	52.78
Gender	Female	Yes	42.86
		No	57.14
	Male	Yes	50.00
		No	50.00
Type of Institution	Govt.	Yes	25.00
		No	75.00
	Aided	Yes	100.00
		No	0.00
	Unaided	Yes	50.00
		No	50.00
Locality	Rural	Yes	0.00
		No	0.00
	Semi-Urban	Yes	25.00
		No	75.00
	Urban	Yes	53.57
		No	46.43
Stream of Degree	Arts	Yes	45.83
		No	54.17
	Science	Yes	50.00
		No	50.00

The data shown in table 4.15 indicates that, for the item O3, 42.86 per cent female and 50.00 per cent male responded yes in gender category, it means more male teacher educators feel that they face difficulty in demonstrating than the female.

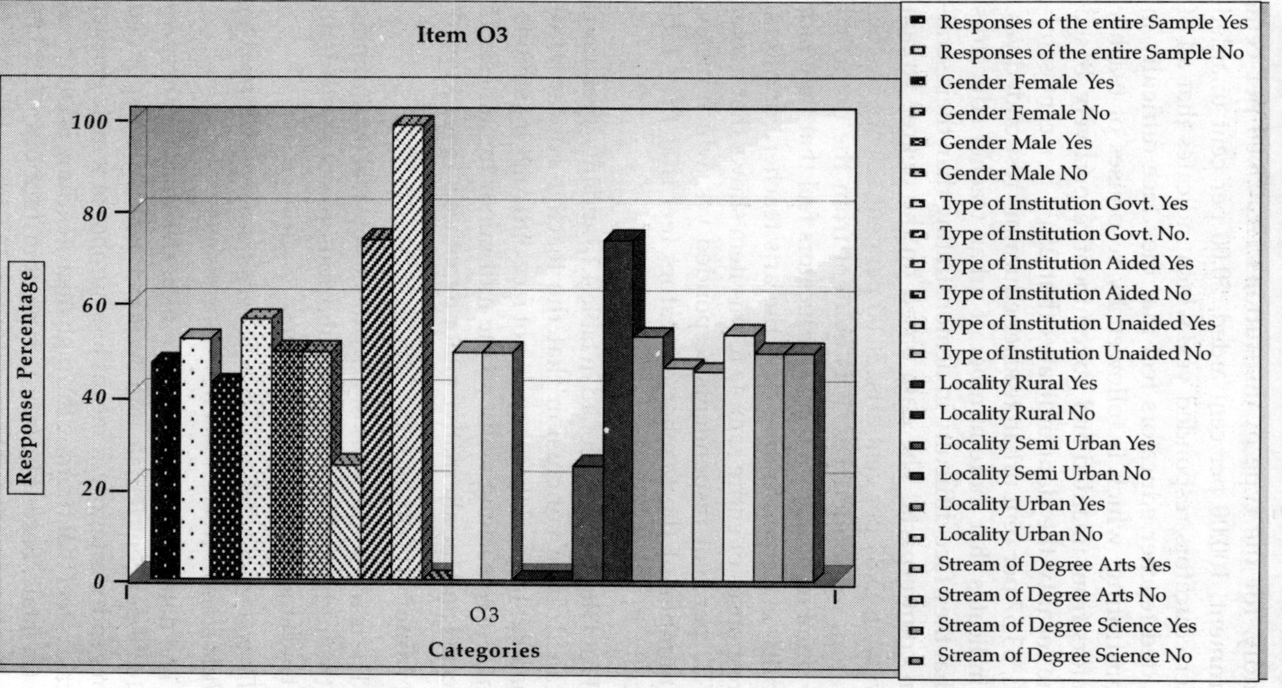

Graph 4.15: **Responses about Facing Difficulty in Demonstrating of Microteaching Skill**

Secondly, for the type of institutions i.e., 25.00 per cent government, 100.00 per cent aided, 50.00 per cent unaided teacher educators responded yes, which indicates that all of the aided teacher educators feel that they face difficulty in demonstrating, which is followed by responses of teacher educators from unaided and government respectively. Based on the locality the data indicates that 25.00 per cent semi-urban, 53.57 per cent urban teacher educators responded yes. This indicates that more number of urban teacher educators feel that they face difficulty in demonstrating than their semi-urban counterparts. The data based on the degree stream shows that 45.83 per cent arts, 50.00 per cent science teacher educators responded yes. It is evident from the data that more number of science teacher educators feel that they face difficulty in demonstrating than the arts teacher educators. The responses of entire sample to this item shows that a total of 47.22 per cent respondents responded yes, which means less number of the teacher educators feel that they face difficulty in demonstrating.

From the data mentioned in table 4.15 and interpretations we can draw a conclusion that the teacher educators of Karnataka state feel that they do not face difficulty in demonstrating microteaching skills, so the null minor hypothesis 15 is rejected and the alternative minor hypothesis 15 is accepted.

Null Minor Hypothesis 16

The teacher educators of Karnataka state feel that training through microteaching is laborious for both student-teachers and their supervisors.

O4: *Do you feel that training through microteaching is laborious for both student-teachers and their supervisors?*

The data shown in table 4.16 indicates that, for the item O4, 14.29 per cent female and 36.36 per cent male responded yes in gender category, it means less number of female teacher educators feel that training through microteaching is laborious than the male. Secondly, for the type of institutions i.e., 25.00 per cent government, 0.00 per cent aided, 30.77 per cent unaided

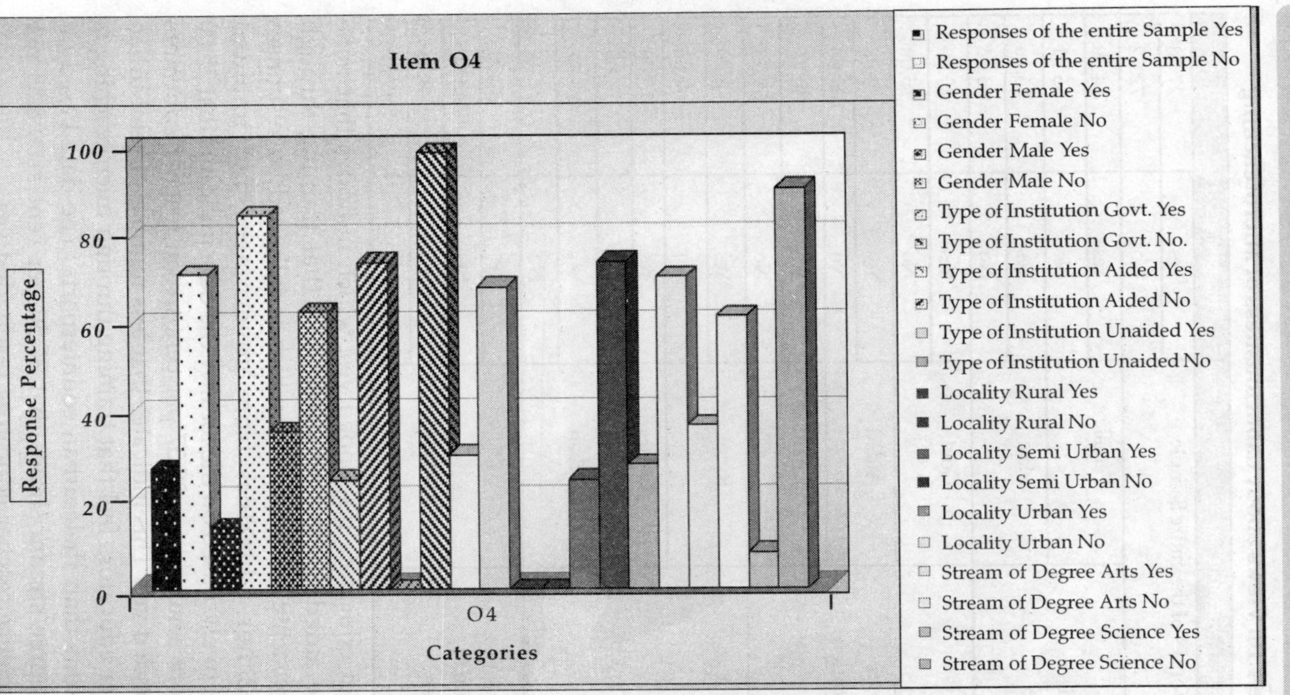

Graph 4.16: Views about Laboriousness of Microteaching

Table 4.16: Views about Laboriousness of Microteaching

Variable		Responses	O4
Responses of the entire Sample		Yes	27.78
		No	72.22
Gender	Female	Yes	14.29
		No	85.71
	Male	Yes	36.36
		No	63.64
Type of Institution	Govt.	Yes	25.00
		No	75.00
	Aided	Yes	0.00
		No	100.00
	Unaided	Yes	30.77
		No	69.23
Locality	Rural	Yes	0.00
		No	0.00
	Semi-Urban	Yes	25.00
		No	75.00
	Urban	Yes	28.57
		No	71.43
Stream of Degree	Arts	Yes	37.50
		No	62.50
	Science	Yes	8.33
		No	91.67

teacher educators responded yes, which indicates that none of the aided teacher educators feel that training through microteaching is laborious, which is followed by responses of teacher educators from government and unaided respectively. Based on the locality the data indicates that 25.00 per cent semi-urban, 28.57 per cent urban teacher educators responded yes. This indicates that less number of semi-urban teacher educators feel that training through microteaching is laborious than their urban counterparts. The data based on the degree stream shows that 37.50 per cent arts, 8.33 per cent science teacher educators responded yes.

It is evident from the data that less number of arts teacher educators feel that training through microteaching is laborious than the science teacher educators. The responses of entire sample to this item shows that a total of only 27.78 per cent respondents responded yes, which means most of the teacher educators do not feel that training through microteaching is laborious.

From the above mentioned data and interpretations we can draw a conclusion that the teacher educators of Karnataka state do not feel that training through microteaching is laborious, so the null minor hypothesis 16 is rejected and the alternative minor hypothesis 16 is accepted.

Null Minor Hypothesis 17

The teacher educators of Karnataka state feel that training through microteaching is time consuming technique.

O5: *Do you feel that training through microteaching is time consuming technique?*

The data shown in table 4.17 indicates that, for the item O5, 28.57 per cent female and 27.27 per cent male responded yes in gender category, it means less number of male teacher educators feel that microteaching is time consuming than the female. Secondly, for the type of institutions i.e., 25.00 per cent government, 0.00 per cent aided, 30.77 per cent unaided teacher educators responded yes, which indicates that none of the aided teacher educators feel that microteaching is time consuming, which is followed by responses of teacher educators from government and unaided respectively. Based on the locality the data indicates that 0.00 per cent semi-urban, 35.71 per cent urban teacher educators responded yes. This indicates that none of the semi-urban teacher educators feel that microteaching is time consuming as compared with their urban counterparts. The data based on the degree stream shows that 33.33 per cent arts, 16.67 per cent science teacher educators responded yes. It is evident from the data that less number of science teacher educators feel that microteaching is time

Table 4.17: Data Show Time Utility of Microteaching

Variable		Responses	O5
Responses of the entire Sample		Yes	27.78
		No	72.22
Gender	Female	Yes	28.57
		No	71.43
	Male	Yes	27.27
		No	72.73
Type of Institution	Govt.	Yes	25.00
		No	75.00
	Aided	Yes	0.00
		No	100.00
	Unaided	Yes	30.77
		No	69.23
Locality	Rural	Yes	0.00
		No	0.00
	Semi-Urban	Yes	0.00
		No	100.00
	Urban	Yes	35.71
		No	64.29
Stream of Degree	Arts	Yes	33.33
		No	66.67
	Science	Yes	16.67
		No	83.33

consuming than the arts teacher educators. The responses of entire sample to this item shows that a total of 27.78 per cent respondents responded yes, which means most of the teacher educators do not feel that microteaching is time consuming.

From the above mentioned data and interpretations we can draw a conclusion that the teacher educators of Karnataka state do not feel that microteaching is time consuming, so the null minor hypothesis 17 is rejected and the alternative minor hypothesis 17 is accepted.

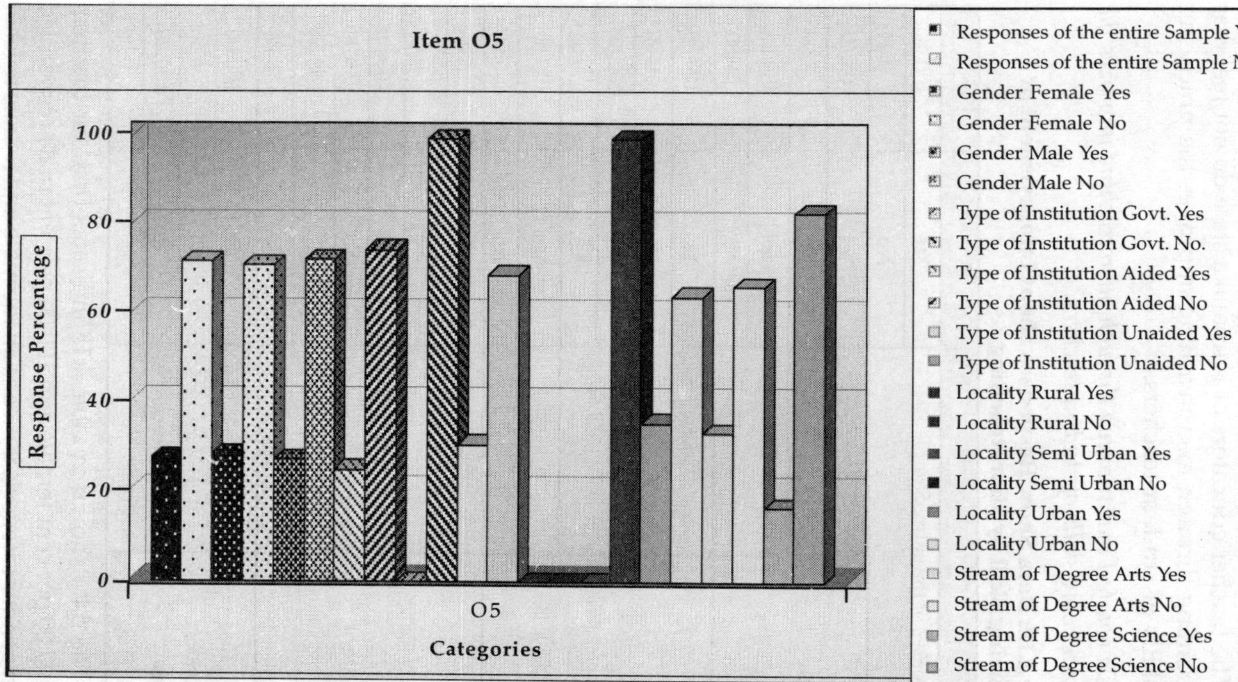

Graph 4.17: **Data Show Time Utility of Microteaching**

Null Minor Hypothesis 18

The teacher educators of Karnataka state do not feel that training through microteaching improves the practicing skills of student-teachers.

O6: *Do you feel that training through microteaching improves the practicing skills of student teachers?*

Table 4.18: Data Show Responses about Improvement of Practicing Skill by Microteaching

Variable		Responses	O6
Responses of the entire Sample		Yes	100.00
		No	0.00
Gender	Female	Yes	100.00
		No	0.00
	Male	Yes	100.00
		No	0.00
Type of Institution	Govt.	Yes	100.00
		No	0.00
	Aided	Yes	100.00
		No	0.00
	Unaided	Yes	100.00
		No	0.00
Locality	Rural	Yes	0.00
		No	0.00
	Semi-Urban	Yes	100.00
		No	0.00
	Urban	Yes	100.00
		No	0.00
Stream of Degree	Arts	Yes	100.00
		No	0.00
	Science	Yes	100.00
		No	0.00

The data shown in table 4.18 indicates that, for the item O6, 100.00 per cent female and 100.00 per cent male responded yes in gender category, it means all the male and female teacher

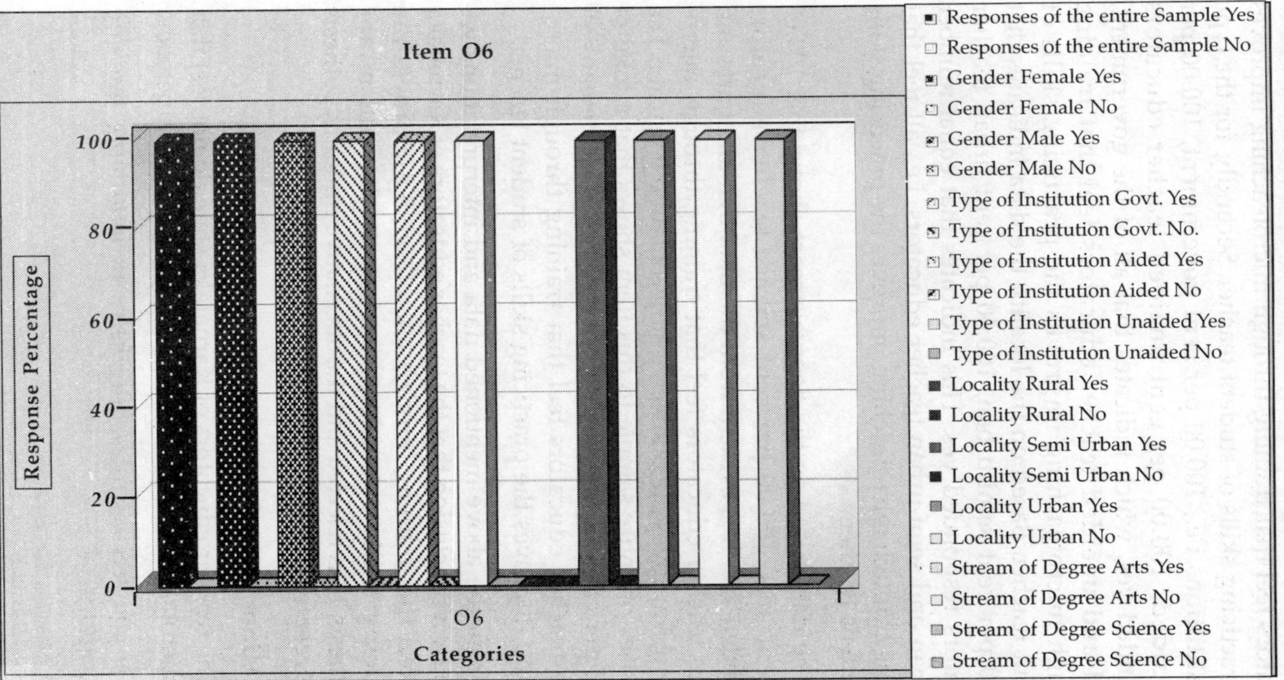

Graph 4.18: **Data Show Responses about Improvement of Practicing Skill by Microteaching**

educators feel that training through microteaching improves the practicing skills of student teacher. Secondly, for the type of institutions i.e., 100.00 per cent government, 100.00 per cent aided, 100.00 per cent unaided teacher educators responded yes, which indicates that all of the government, aided and unaided teacher educators feel that training through microteaching improves the practicing skills of student teacher. Based on the locality the data indicates that 100.00 per cent semi-urban, 100.00 per cent urban teacher educators responded yes. This indicates that equal number of urban and semi-urban teacher educators, i.e., all feel that training through microteaching improves the practicing skills of student teacher.

The data based on the degree stream shows that 100.00 per cent arts, 100.00 per cent science teacher educators responded yes. It is evident from the data that all of arts and science teacher educators feel that training through microteaching improves the practicing skills of student teacher. The responses of entire sample to this item shows that a total of 100.00 per cent respondents responded yes, which means all of the teacher educators feel that training through microteaching improves the practicing skills of student teacher.

From the above mentioned data and interpretations we can draw a conclusion that the teacher educators of Karnataka state feel that training through microteaching improves the practicing skills of student teacher, so the null minor hypothesis 18 is rejected and the alternative minor hypothesis 18 is accepted.

Null Minor Hypothesis 19

The teacher educators of Karnataka state do not feel that microteaching helps in improving teaching competency.

O7: *Do you feel microteaching helps in improving teaching competency?*

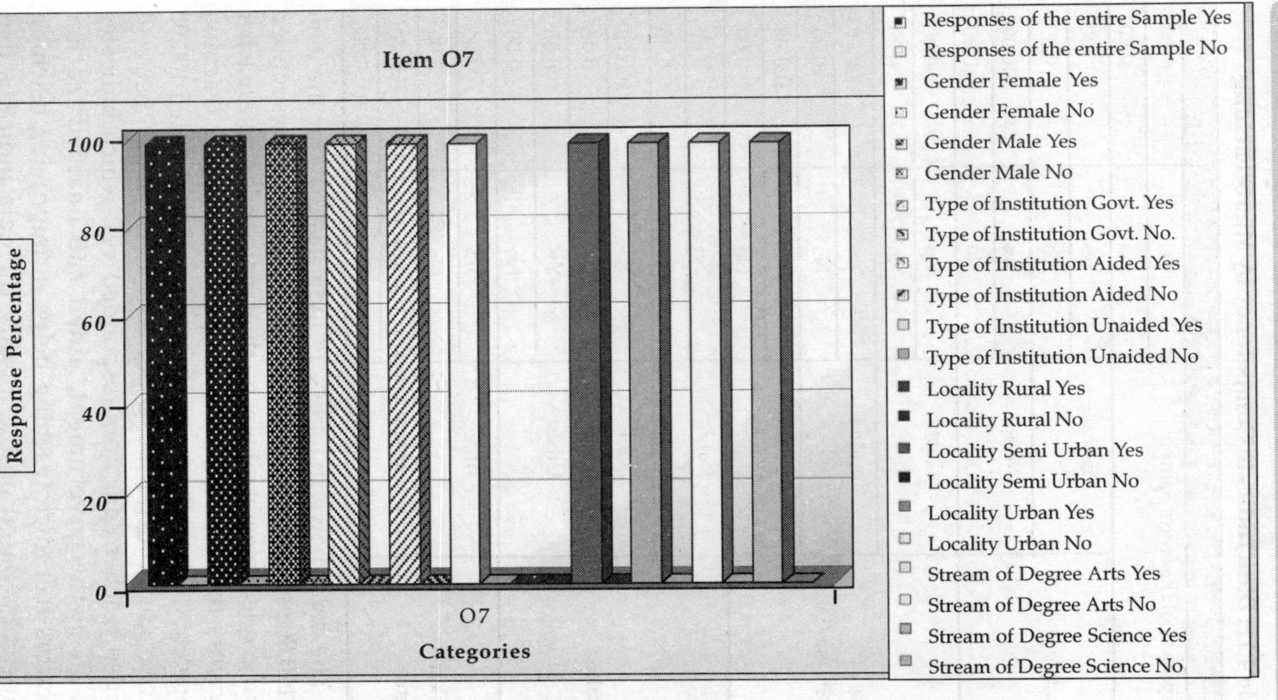

Graph 4.19: **Data Indicate Teaching Competency by Microteaching**

Table 4.19: Data Indicate Competency by Microteaching

Variable		Responses	O7
Responses of the entire Sample		Yes	100.00
		No	0.00
Gender	Female	Yes	100.00
		No	0.00
	Male	Yes	100.00
		No	0.00
Type of Institution	Govt.	Yes	100.00
		No	0.00
	Aided	Yes	100.00
		No	0.00
	Unaided	Yes	100.00
		No	0.00
Locality	Rural	Yes	0.00
		No	0.00
	Semi-Urban	Yes	100.00
		No	0.00
	Urban	Yes	100.00
		No	0.00
Stream of Degree	Arts	Yes	100.00
		No	0.00
	Science	Yes	100.00
		No	0.00

The data shown in table 4.19 indicates that, for the item O7, 100.00 per cent female and 100.00 per cent male responded yes in gender category, it means all of male and female teacher educators feel microteaching helps in improving teaching competency. Secondly, for the type of institutions i.e., 100.00 per cent government, 100.00 per cent aided, 100.00 per cent unaided teacher educators responded yes, which indicates that all of the government, aided and unaided teacher educators feel microteaching helps in improving teaching competency. Based on the locality the data indicates that

100.00 per cent semi-urban, 100.00 per cent urban teacher educators responded yes. This indicates that all urban and semi-urban teacher educators feel microteaching helps in improving teaching competency. The data based on the degree stream shows that 100.00 per cent arts, 100.00 per cent science teacher educators responded yes. It is evident from the data that all the arts and science teacher educators feel microteaching helps in improving teaching competency. The responses of entire sample to this item shows that a total of 100.00 per cent respondents responded yes, which means all the teacher educators feel microteaching helps in improving teaching competency.

From the above mentioned data and interpretations we can draw a conclusion that the teacher educators of Karnataka state feel microteaching helps in improving teaching competency, so the null minor hypothesis 19 is rejected and the alternative minor hypothesis 19 is accepted.

Null Minor Hypothesis 20

The teacher educators of Karnataka state do not think that observation play an important role in microteaching.

O8: *Do you think that observation plays an important role in microteaching?*

The data shown in table 4.20 indicates that, for the item O8, 100.00 per cent female and 100.00 per cent male responded yes in gender category, it means all of male and female teacher educators think that observation plays an important role in learning microteaching. Secondly, for the type of institutions i.e., 100.00 per cent government, 100.00 per cent aided, 100.00 per cent unaided teacher educators responded yes, which indicates that all of the government, aided and unaided teacher educators think that observation plays an important role in learning microteaching. Based on the locality the data indicates that 100.00 per cent semi-urban, 100.00 per cent urban teacher educators responded yes. This indicates that all urban and semi-urban teacher educators think that observation plays an important role in learning microteaching. The data based

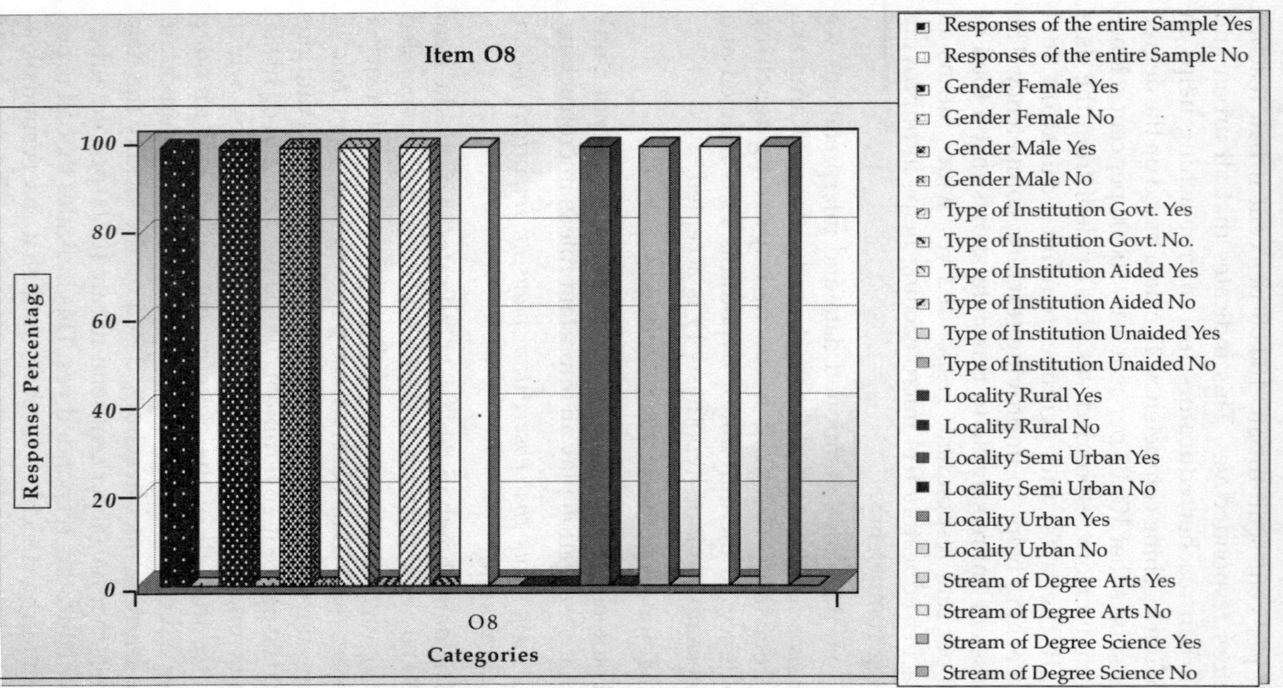

Graph 4.20: **Data for Observation in Microteaching**

Table 4.20: Data for Observation in Microteaching

Variable		Responses	O8
Responses of the entire Sample		Yes	100.00
		No	0.00
Gender	Female	Yes	100.00
		No	0.00
	Male	Yes	100.00
		No	0.00
Type of Institution	Govt.	Yes	100.00
		No	0.00
	Aided	Yes	100.00
		No	0.00
	Unaided	Yes	100.00
		No	0.00
Locality	Rural	Yes	0.00
		No	0.00
	Semi-Urban	Yes	100.00
		No	0.00
	Urban	Yes	100.00
		No	0.00
Stream of Degree	Arts	Yes	100.00
		No	0.00
	Science	Yes	100.00
		No	0.00

on the degree stream shows that 100.00 per cent arts, 100.00 per cent science teacher educators responded yes. It is evident from the data that all the arts and science teacher educators think that observation plays an important role in learning microteaching. The responses of entire sample to this item shows that a total of 100.00 per cent respondents responded yes, which means all the teacher educators think that observation plays an important role in learning microteaching.

From the above mentioned data and interpretations we can draw a conclusion that the teacher educators of Karnataka state think that observation plays an important role in learning microteaching, so the null minor hypothesis 20 is rejected and the alternative minor hypothesis 20 is accepted.

Null Minor Hypothesis 21

The teacher educators of Karnataka state do not think that feedback helps in improving the skills.

O9: *Do you think that feedback helps in improving the skills?*

Table 4.21: Responses about the Help of Feedback in Improving the Skill

Variable		Responses	O9
Responses of the entire Sample		Yes	100.00
		No	0.00
Gender	Female	Yes	100.00
		No	0.00
	Male	Yes	100.00
		No	0.00
Type of Institution	Govt.	Yes	100.00
		No	0.00
	Aided	Yes	100.00
		No	0.00
	Unaided	Yes	100.00
		No	0.00
Locality	Rural	Yes	0.00
		No	0.00
	Semi-Urban	Yes	100.00
		No	0.00
	Urban	Yes	100.00
		No	0.00
Stream of Degree	Arts	Yes	100.00
		No	0.00
	Science	Yes	100.00
		No	0.00

The data shown in table 4.21 indicates that, for the item O9, 100.00 per cent female and 100.00 per cent male responded yes in gender category, it means all of male and female teacher educators think that feedback helps in improving the skills.

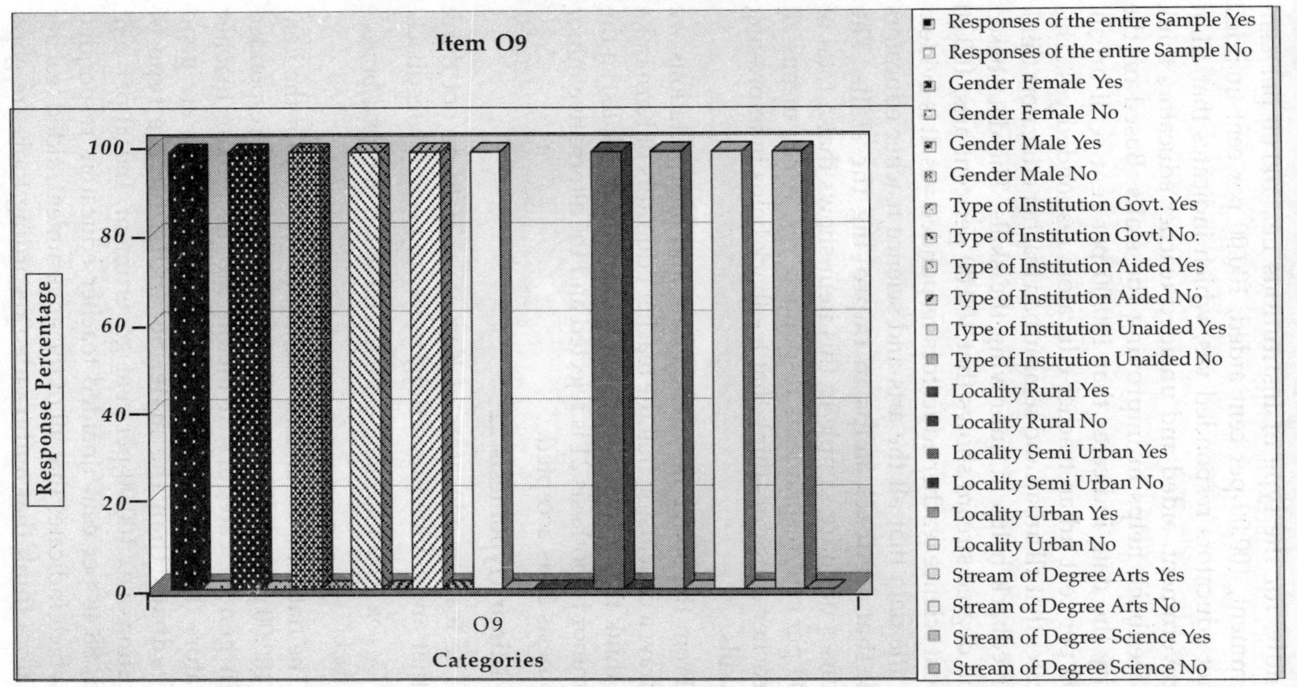

Graph 4.21: **Responses about the Help of Feedback in Improving the of Skill**

Secondly, for the type of institutions i.e., 100.00 per cent government, 100.00 per cent aided, 100.00 per cent unaided teacher educators responded yes, which indicates that all of the government, aided and unaided teacher educators think that feedback helps in improving the skills. Based on the locality the data indicates that 100.00 per cent semi-urban, 100.00 per cent urban teacher educators responded yes. This indicates that all urban and semi-urban teacher educators think that feedback helps in improving the skills. The data based on the degree stream shows that 100.00 per cent arts, 100.00 per cent science teacher educators responded yes. It is evident from the data that all the arts and science teacher educators think that feedback helps in improving the skills. The responses of entire sample to this item shows that a total of 100.00 per cent respondents responded yes, which means all the teacher educators think that feedback helps in improving the skills.

From the above mentioned data and interpretations we can draw a conclusion that the teacher educators of Karnataka state think that feedback helps in improving the skills, so the null minor hypothesis 21 is rejected and the alternative minor hypothesis 21 is accepted.

Null Minor Hypothesis 22

The teacher educators of Karnataka state do not think that audio-video recording tools are good for feedback.

O10: *Do you think that audio-video recording tools are good for feedback?*

The data shown in table 4.22 indicates that, for the item O10, 100.00 per cent female and 86.36 per cent male responded yes in gender category, it means all the female teacher educators think that audio-video recording tools are good for feedback than the male. Secondly, for the type of institutions i.e., 100.00 per cent government, 100.00 per cent aided, 88.46 per cent unaided teacher educators responded yes, which indicates that all of the government, aided teacher educators think that audio-video recording tools are good

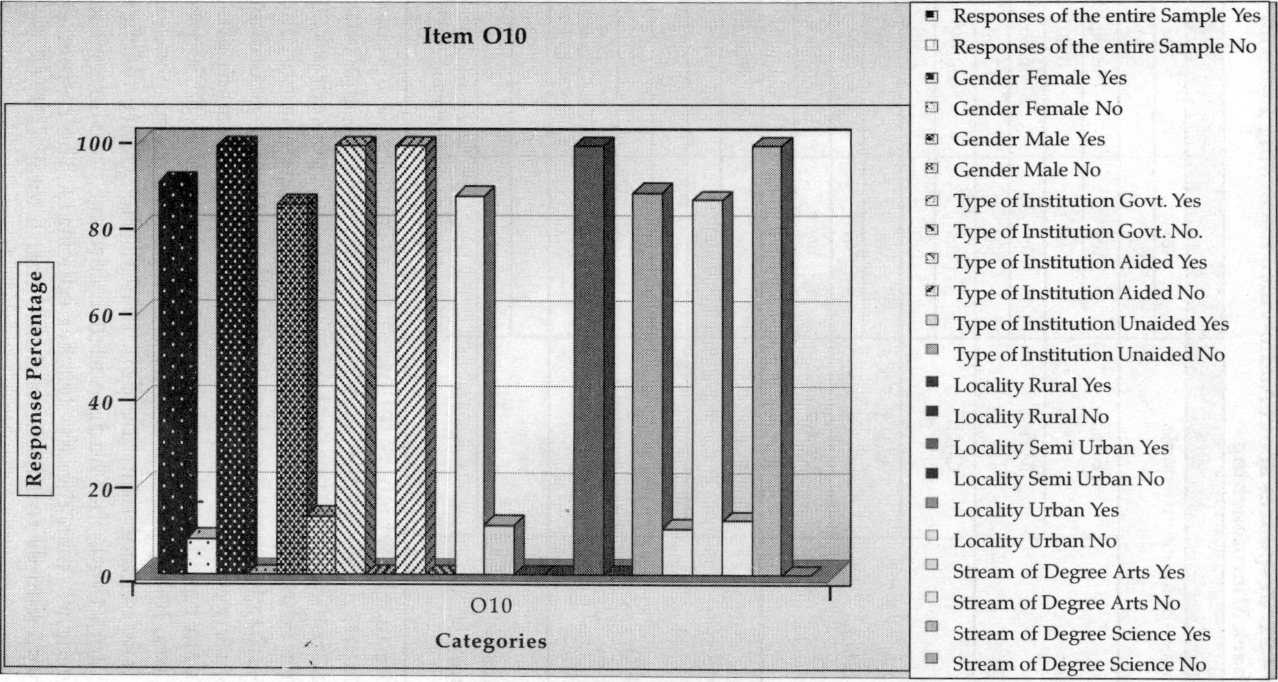

Graph 4.22: **Responses about Audio-video Recording Tools for Feedback Microteaching**

Table 4.22: Responses about Audio-video Recording Tool's for Feedback Microteaching

Variable		Responses	O10
Responses of the entire Sample		Yes	91.67
		No	8.33
Gender	Female	Yes	100.00
		No	0.00
	Male	Yes	86.36
		No	13.64
Type of Institution	Govt.	Yes	100.00
		No	0.00
	Aided	Yes	100.00
		No	0.00
	Unaided	Yes	88.64
		No	11.54
Locality	Rural	Yes	0.00
		No	0.00
	Semi-Urban	Yes	100.00
		No	0.00
	Urban	Yes	89.29
		No	10.71
Stream of Degree	Arts	Yes	87.50
		No	12.50
	Science	Yes	100.00
		No	0.00

for feedback, which is followed by responses of teacher educators from unaided. Based on the locality the data indicates that 100.00 per cent semi-urban, 89.29 per cent urban teacher educators responded yes. This indicates that all the semi-urban teacher educators think that audio-video recording tools are good for feedback than their urban counterparts. The data based on the degree stream shows that 87.50 per cent arts, 100.00 per cent science teacher educators responded yes. It is evident from the data that all the science teacher educators think that audio-video recording tools are good for feedback than the arts teacher educators. The responses of entire sample to this item shows that a total of 91.67 per cent respondents responded yes, which means most of the teacher educators think that audio-video recording tools are good for feedback.

From the above mentioned data and interpretations we can draw a conclusion that the teacher educators of Karnataka state think that audio-video recording tools are good for feedback, so the null minor hypothesis O10 is rejected and the alternative minor hypothesis O10 is accepted.

Null Minor Hypothesis 23

The teacher educators of Karnataka state do not think that microteaching gradually teaches integration of various teaching skills.

O11: *Do you think that microteaching gradually teaches integration of various teaching skills?*

Table 4.23: Data Show Integration of Skills by Microteaching

Variable		Responses	O11
Responses of the entire Sample		Yes	94.44
		No	5.56
Gender	Female	Yes	100.00
		No	0.00
	Male	Yes	90.91
		No	9.09
Type of Institution	Govt.	Yes	87.50
		No	12.50
	Aided	Yes	100.00
		No	0.00
	Unaided	Yes	96.15
		No	3.85
Locality	Rural	Yes	0.00
		No	0.00
	Semi-Urban	Yes	87.50
		No	12.50
	Urban	Yes	96.43
		No	3.57
Stream of Degree	Arts	Yes	91.67
		No	8.33
	Science	Yes	100.00
		No	0.00

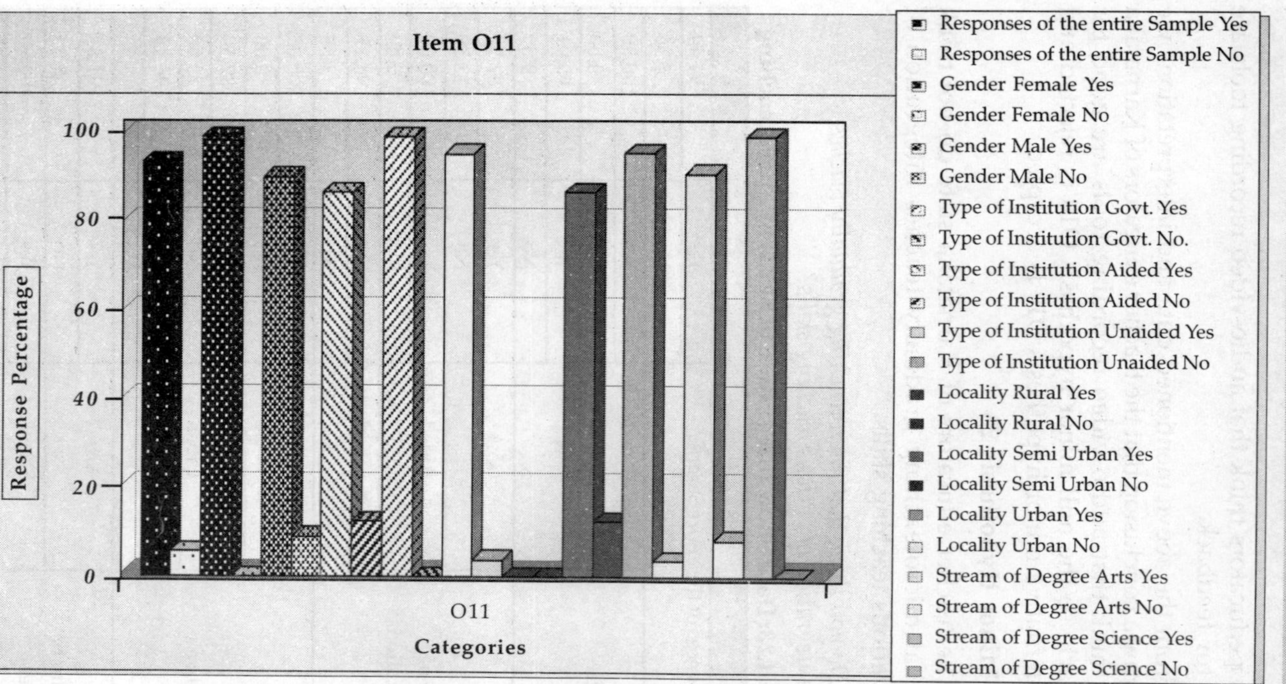

Graph 4.23: **Data Indicate Integration of Skills by Microteaching**

The data shown in table 4.23 indicates that, for the item O11, 100.00 per cent female and 90.91 per cent male responded yes in gender category, it means all of female teacher educators think that microteaching gradually teaches integration of various teaching skills than the male. Secondly, for the type of institutions i.e., 87.50 per cent government, 100.00 per cent aided, 96.15 per cent unaided teacher educators responded yes, which indicates that all of the aided teacher educators think that microteaching gradually teaches integration of various teaching skills, which is followed by responses of teacher educators from unaided and government respectively.

Based on the locality the data indicates that 87.50 per cent semi-urban, 96.43 per cent urban teacher educators responded yes. This indicates that more number of urban teacher educators think that microteaching gradually teaches integration of various teaching skills than their semi-urban counterparts. The data based on the degree stream shows that 91.67 per cent arts, 100.00 per cent science teacher educators responded yes. It is evident from the data that all the science teacher educators think that microteaching gradually teaches integration of various teaching skills than the arts teacher educators. The responses of entire sample to this item shows that a total of 94.44 per cent respondents responded yes, which means most of the teacher educators think that microteaching gradually teaches integration of various teaching skills.

From the above mentioned data and interpretations we can draw a conclusion that the teacher educators of Karnataka state think that microteaching gradually teaches integration of various teaching skills, so the null minor hypothesis 23 is rejected and the alternative minor hypothesis 23 is accepted.

Null Minor Hypothesis 24

The teacher educators of Karnataka state feel that student-teachers feel boredom during practice of teaching skills.

O12: *Do you feel that student-teachers feel boredom during practice of teaching skills?*

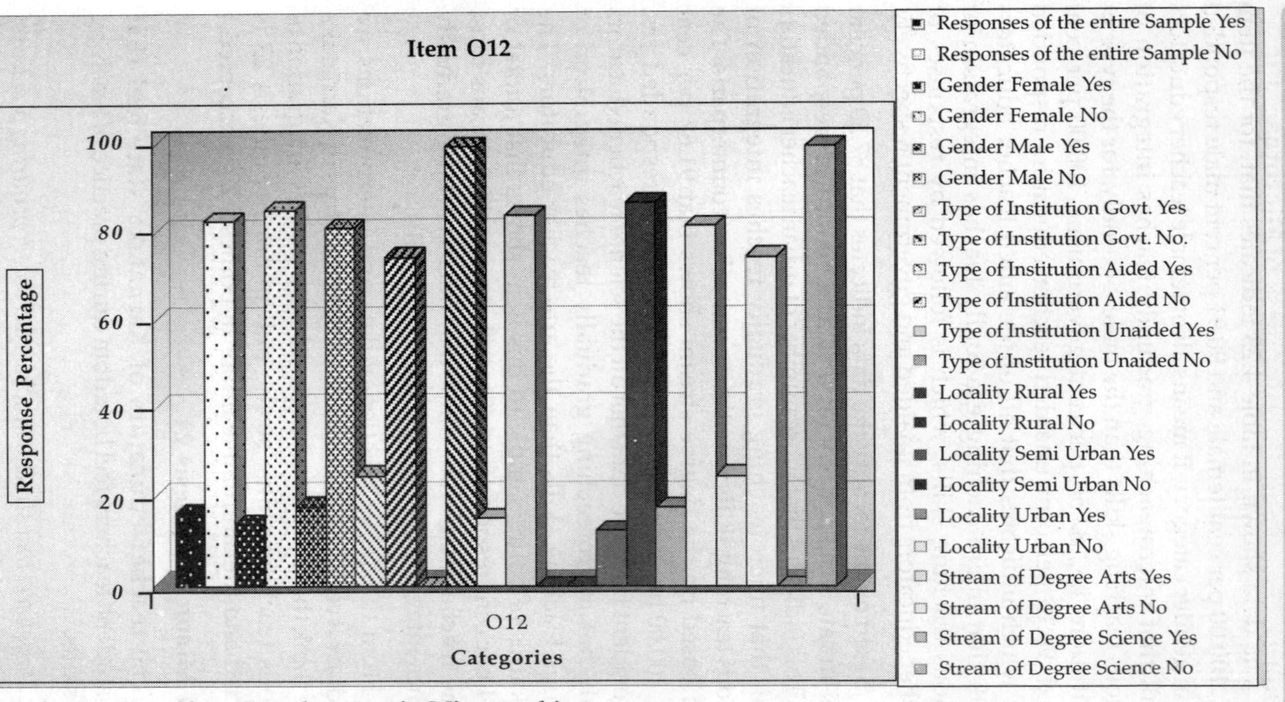

Graph 4.24: Data Show Boredomness in Microteaching

Table 4.24: Data Show Boredomness in Microteaching

Variable		Responses	O12
Responses of the entire Sample		Yes	16.67
		No	83.33
Gender	Female	Yes	14.29
		No	85.71
	Male	Yes	18.18
		No	81.82
Type of Institution	Govt.	Yes	25.00
		No	75.00
	Aided	Yes	0.00
		No	100.00
	Unaided	Yes	15.38
		No	84.62
Locality	Rural	Yes	0.00
		No	0.00
	Semi-Urban	Yes	12.50
		No	87.50
	Urban	Yes	17.86
		No	82.14
Stream of Degree	Arts	Yes	25.00
		No	75.00
	Science	Yes	0.00
		No	100.00

The data shown in table 4.24 indicates that, for the item O12, 14.29 per cent female and 18.18 per cent male responded yes in gender category, it means less number of female teacher educators feel that student-teachers feel boredom during practice of teaching skills than the male. Secondly, for the type of institutions i.e., 25.00 per cent government, 0.00 per cent aided, 15.38 per cent unaided teacher educators responded yes, which indicates that none of the aided teacher educators feel that student-teachers feel boredom during practice of teaching skills, which is followed by responses of teacher educator from unaided and government respectively.

Based on the locality the data indicates that 12.50 per cent semi-urban, 17.86 per cent urban teacher educators responded yes. This indicates that less number of semi-urban teacher educators feel that student-teachers feel boredom during practice of teaching skills than their urban counterparts. The data based on the degree stream shows that 25.00 per cent arts, 0.00 per cent science teacher educators responded yes. It is evident from the data that none of the science teacher educators feel that student-teachers feel boredom during practice of teaching skills than the science/arts teacher educators. The responses of entire sample to this item shows that a total of 16.67 per cent respondents responded yes, which means very less number of the teacher educators feel that student-teachers feel boredom during practice of teaching skills.

From the above mentioned data and interpretations we can draw a conclusion that the teacher educators of Karnataka state feel that student-teachers feel boredom during practice of teaching skills, so the null minor hypothesis 24 is rejected and the alternative minor hypothesis 24 is accepted.

Null Minor Hypothesis 25

The teacher educators of Karnataka state do not agree that their student teachers practice microteaching skills in accordance with microteaching cycle.

O13: *Do your student-teachers practice microteaching skills in accordance with microteaching cycle?*

The data shown in table 4.25 indicates that, for the item O13, 100.00 per cent female and 90.91 per cent male responded yes in gender category, it means all of the female teacher educators agree that the student-teachers practice micro-teaching skills in accordance with microteaching cycle than the male. Secondly, for the type of institutions i.e., 100.00 per cent government, 100.00 per cent aided, 92.31 per cent unaided teacher educators responded yes, which indicates that all of the government and aided teacher educators agree that the student-teachers practice microteaching skills in accordance with microteaching cycle, which is followed by responses of teacher educators from unaided. Based on the locality the data indicates that 75.00 per cent semi-urban, 100.00 per cent urban teacher educators responded yes.

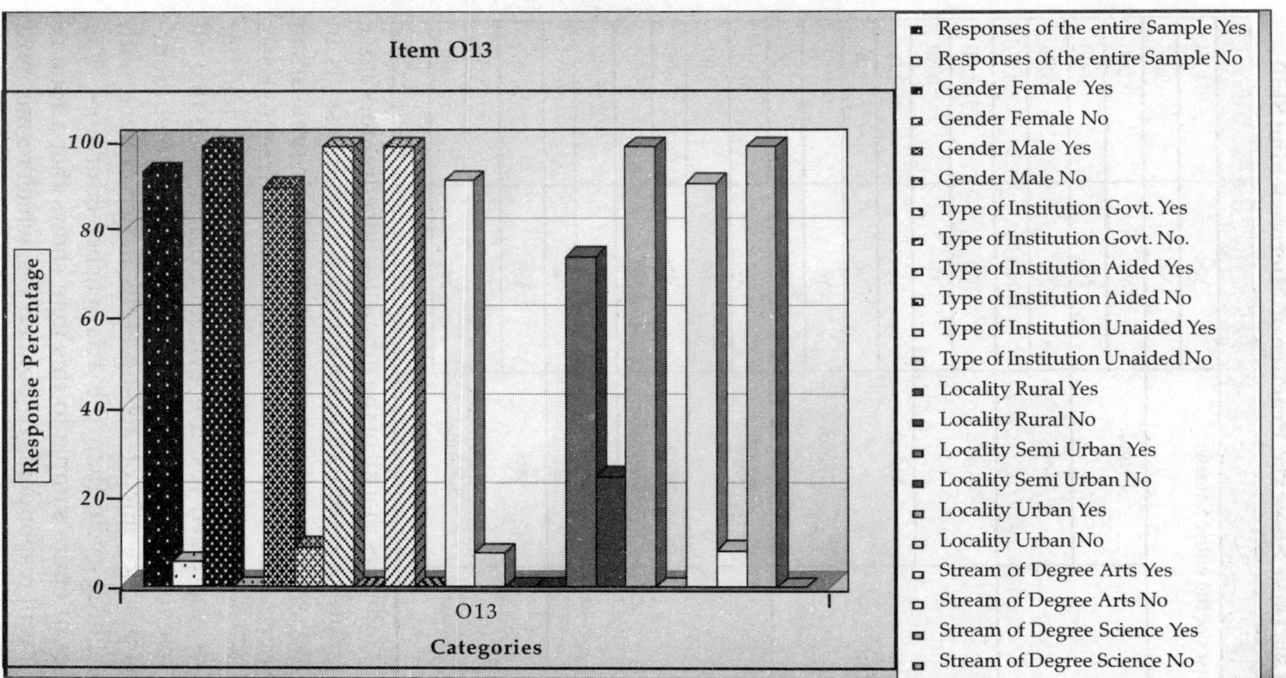

Graph 4.25: **Data Show the Practice of Microteaching Skills**

Table 4.25: Data Show the Practice of Microteaching Skill

Variable		Responses	O13
Responses of the entire Sample		Yes	94.44
		No	5.56
Gender	Female	Yes	100.00
		No	0.00
	Male	Yes	90.91
		No	9.09
Type of Institution	Govt.	Yes	100.00
		No	0.00
	Aided	Yes	100.00
		No	0.00
	Unaided	Yes	92.31
		No	7.69
Locality	Rural	Yes	0.00
		No	0.00
	Semi-Urban	Yes	75.00
		No	25.00
	Urban	Yes	100.00
		No	0.00
Stream of Degree	Arts	Yes	91.67
		No	8.33
	Science	Yes	100.00
		No	0.00

This indicates that all of the urban teacher educators agree that the student-teachers practice microteaching skills in accordance with microteaching cycle than their semi-urban counterparts. The data based on the degree stream shows that 91.67 per cent arts, 100.00 per cent science teacher educators responded yes. It is evident from the data that all of the science teacher educators agree that the student-teachers practice microteaching skills in accordance with microteaching cycle than the arts teacher educators. The responses of entire sample to this item shows that a total of 94.44 per cent respondents responded yes, which means most of the teacher educators agree that the student-teachers practice microteaching skills in accordance with microteaching cycle.

From the above mentioned data and interpretations we can draw a conclusion that the teacher educators of Karnataka state agree that the student-teachers practice microteaching skills in accordance with microteaching cycle, so the null minor hypothesis 25 is rejected and the alternative minor hypothesis 25 is accepted.

Null Minor Hypothesis 26

The teacher educators of Karnataka state do not agree that their student teachers perform the microteaching enthusiastically.

O14: *Do your student-teacher perform the microteaching enthusiastically?*

The data shown in table 4.26 indicates that, for the item O14, 100.00 per cent female and 100.00 per cent male responded yes in gender category, it means all of male and female teacher educators agree that their student-teacher perform the microteaching enthusiastically. Secondly, for the type of institutions i.e., 100.00 per cent government, 100.00 per cent aided, 100.00 per cent unaided teacher educators responded yes, which indicates that all of the government, aided and unaided teacher educators agree that their student-teacher perform the microteaching enthusiastically. Based on the locality the data indicates that 100.00 per cent semi-urban, 100.00 per cent urban teacher educators responded yes. This indicates that all urban and semi-urban teacher educators agree that their student-teacher perform the microteaching enthusiastically. The data based on the degree stream shows that 100.00 per cent arts, 100.00 per cent science teacher educators responded yes. It is evident from the data that all the arts and science teacher educators agree that their student-teacher perform the microteaching enthusiastically. The responses of entire sample to this item shows that a total of 100.00 per cent respondents responded yes, which means all the teacher educators agree that their student-teacher perform the microteaching enthusiastically.

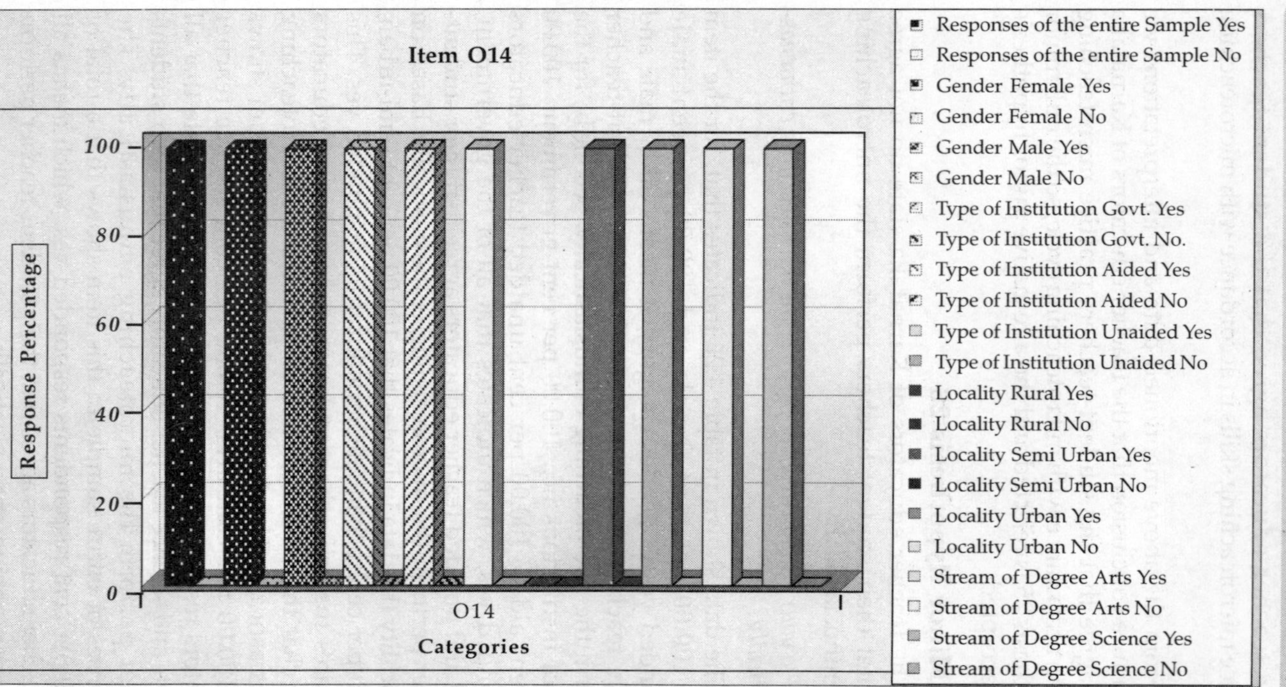

Graph 4.26: **Data Show the Performance of Microteaching Skill by Student Teachers**

Table 4.26: Data Show the Performance of Microteaching Skill by Student Teachers

Variable		Responses	O14
Responses of the entire Sample		Yes	100.00
		No	0.00
Gender	Female	Yes	100.00
		No	0.00
	Male	Yes	100.00
		No	0.00
Type of Institution	Govt.	Yes	100.00
		No	0.00
	Aided	Yes	100.00
		No	0.00
	Unaided	Yes	100.00
		No	0.00
Locality	Rural	Yes	0.00
		No	0.00
	Semi-Urban	Yes	100.00
		No	0.00
	Urban	Yes	100.00
		No	0.00
Stream of Degree	Arts	Yes	100.00
		No	0.00
	Science	Yes	100.00
		No	0.00

From the above mentioned data and interpretations we can draw a conclusion that the teacher educators of Karnataka state agree that their student-teacher perform the microteaching enthusiastically, so the null minor hypothesis 26 is rejected and the alternative minor hypothesis 26 is accepted.

Null Minor Hypothesis 27

The teacher educators of Karnataka state do not teach minimum of 6 microteaching skills to their students.

O15: *Do you teach minimum of 6 microteaching skills to your students?*

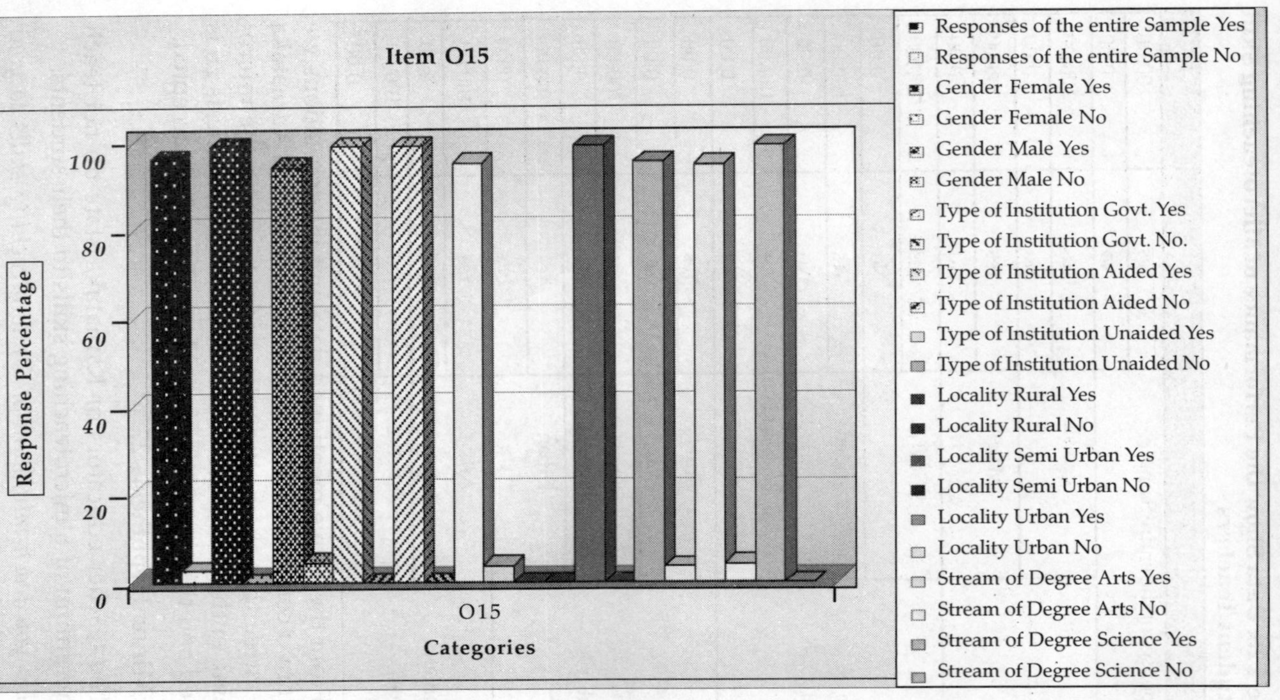

Graph 4.27: **Data Show the Number of Practicing Skills of Microteaching**

Table 4.27: Data Show the Number of Practicing Skills of Microteaching

Variable		Responses	O15
Responses of the entire Sample		Yes	97.22
		No	2.78
Gender	Female	Yes	100.00
		No	0.00
	Male	Yes	95.45
		No	4.55
Type of Institution	Govt.	Yes	100.00
		No	0.00
	Aided	Yes	100.00
		No	0.00
	Unaided	Yes	96.15
		No	3.85
Locality	Rural	Yes	0.00
		No	0.00
	Semi-Urban	Yes	100.00
		No	0.00
	Urban	Yes	96.43
		No	3.57
Stream of Degree	Arts	Yes	95.83
		No	4.17
	Science	Yes	100.00
		No	0.00

The data shown in table 4.27 indicates that, for the item O15, 100.00 per cent female and 95.45 per cent male responded yes in gender category, it means all of the female teacher educators agree that they teach minimum of 6 microteaching skills to their students than the male/female. Secondly, for the type of institutions i.e., 100.00 per cent government, 100.00 per cent aided, 96.15 per cent unaided teacher educators responded yes, which indicates that all of the government, aided teacher educators agree that they teach minimum of 6 microteaching skills to their students, which is followed by responses of teacher educators from unaided. Based on the locality the data indicates that 100.00 per cent semi-urban, 96.43 per cent urban teacher educators responded yes. This indicates that all the semi-urban teacher educators agree that they teach minimum of 6 microteaching skills to their students than their urban counterparts. The data based on the degree stream shows that 95.83 per cent arts, 100.00 per cent science teacher educators responded yes. It is evident from the data that all of the science teacher educators agree that they teach minimum of 6 microteaching skills to their students than the arts teacher educators. The responses of entire sample to this item shows that a total of 97.22 per cent respondents responded yes, which means most of the teacher educators agree that they teach minimum of 6 microteaching skills to their students.

From the above mentioned data and interpretations we can draw a conclusion that the teacher educators of Karnataka state agree that they teach minimum of 6 microteaching skills to their students, so the null minor hypothesis 27 is rejected and the alternative minor hypothesis 27 is accepted.

Null Minor Hypothesis 28

The teacher educators of Karnataka state do not agree that student teachers practice at least 6 microteaching skills.

O16: *Do your student-teachers perform at least 6 microteaching skills?*

The data shown in table 4.28 indicates that, for the item O16, 100.00 per cent female and 95.45 per cent male responded yes in gender category, it means all of the female teacher educators agree that their student-teachers perform at least 6 microteaching skills than the male. Secondly, for the type of institutions i.e., 100.00 per cent government, 100.00 per cent aided, 96.15 per cent unaided teacher educators responded yes, which indicates that all of the government and aided teacher educators agree that their student-teachers perform at least 6 microteaching skills, which is followed by responses

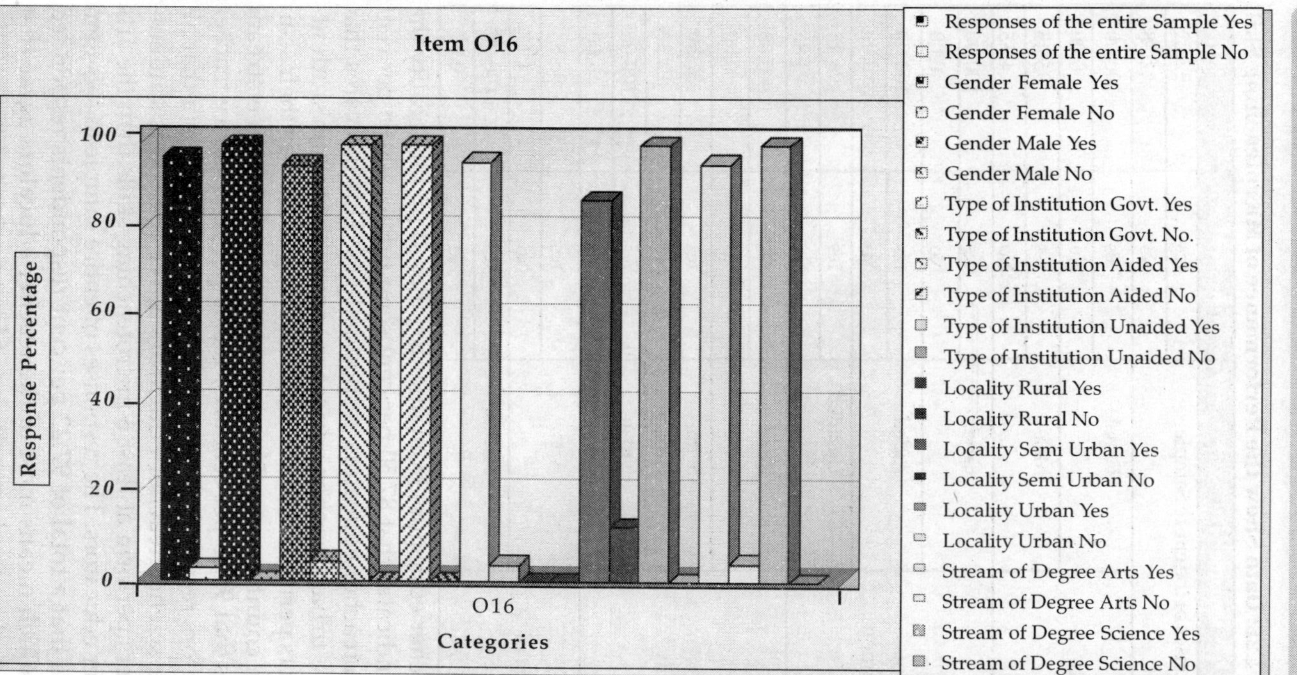

Graph 4.28: **Data Show the Performance of Microteaching Skill**

Table 4.28: Data Show the Performance of Microteaching Skill

Variable		Responses	O16
Responses of the entire Sample		Yes	97.22
		No	2.78
Gender	Female	Yes	100.00
		No	0.00
	Male	Yes	95.45
		No	4.55
Type of Institution	Govt.	Yes	100.00
		No	0.00
	Aided	Yes	100.00
		No	0.00
	Unaided	Yes	96.15
		No	3.85
Locality	Rural	Yes	0.00
		No	0.00
	Semi-Urban	Yes	87.50
		No	12.50
	Urban	Yes	100.00
		No	0.00
Stream of Degree	Arts	Yes	95.83
		No	4.17
	Science	Yes	100.00
		No	0.00

of teacher educators from unaided. Based on the locality the data indicates that 87.50 per cent semi-urban, 100.00 per cent urban teacher educators responded yes. This indicates that all the urban teacher educators agree that their student-teachers perform at least 6 microteaching skills than their semi urban counterparts. The data based on the degree stream shows that 95.83 per cent arts, 100.00 per cent science teacher educators responded yes. It is evident from the data that all of the science teacher educators agree that their student-teachers perform at least 6 microteaching skills than the arts teacher educators. The responses of entire sample to this item shows that a total of 97.22 per cent respondents responded yes, which means most of the teacher educators agree that their student-teachers perform at least 6 microteaching skills.

From the above mentioned data and interpretations we can draw a conclusion that the teacher educators of Karnataka state agree that their student-teachers perform at least 6 microteaching skills, so the null minor hypothesis 28 is rejected and the alternative minor hypothesis 28 is accepted.

Null Minor Hypothesis 29

The teacher educators of Karnataka state think that student teachers want to go for practice teaching directly without undergoing microteaching.

O17: *Do you think that student-teachers want to go for practice teaching directly without undergoing microteaching?*

The data shown in table 4.29 indicates that, for the item O17, 21.43 per cent female and 9.09 per cent male responded yes in gender category, it means less number of male teacher educators think that the student-teachers want to practice teaching directly without undergoing microteaching than the female. Secondly, for the type of institutions i.e., 25.00 per cent government, 0.00 per cent aided, 11.54 per cent unaided teacher educators responded yes, which indicates that none of the aided teacher educators think that the student-teachers want to practice teaching directly without undergoing microteaching, which is followed by responses of teacher educators from unaided and government respectively. Based on the locality the data indicates that 0.00 per cent semi-urban, 17.86 per cent urban teacher educators responded yes. This indicates that none of semi-urban teacher educators think that the student-teachers want to practice teaching directly without undergoing microteaching than their urban counterparts. The data based on the degree stream shows that 20.83 per cent arts, 0.00 per cent science teacher educators responded yes. It is evident from the data that none of science teacher educators think that the student-teachers want to practice teaching directly without undergoing microteaching than the arts teacher educators.

Table 4.29: Data Show Usage of Microteaching

Variable		Responses	O17
Responses of the entire Sample		Yes	13.89
		No	86.11
Gender	Female	Yes	21.43
		No	78.57
	Male	Yes	9.09
		No	90.91
Type of Institution	Govt.	Yes	25.00
		No	75.00
	Aided	Yes	0.00
		No	100.00
	Unaided	Yes	11.54
		No	88.46
Locality	Rural	Yes	0.00
		No	0.00
	Semi-Urban	Yes	0.00
		No	100.00
	Urban	Yes	17.86
		No	82.14
Stream of Degree	Arts	Yes	20.83
		No	79.17
	Science	Yes	0.00
		No	100.00

The responses of entire sample to this item shows that a total of 13.89 per cent respondents responded yes, which means most of the teacher educators do not think that the student-teachers want to practice teaching directly without undergoing microteaching.

From the above mentioned data and interpretations we can draw a conclusion that the teacher educators of Karnataka state do not think that the student-teachers want to practice teaching directly without undergoing microteaching, so the null minor hypothesis 29 is rejected and the alternative minor hypothesis 29 is accepted.

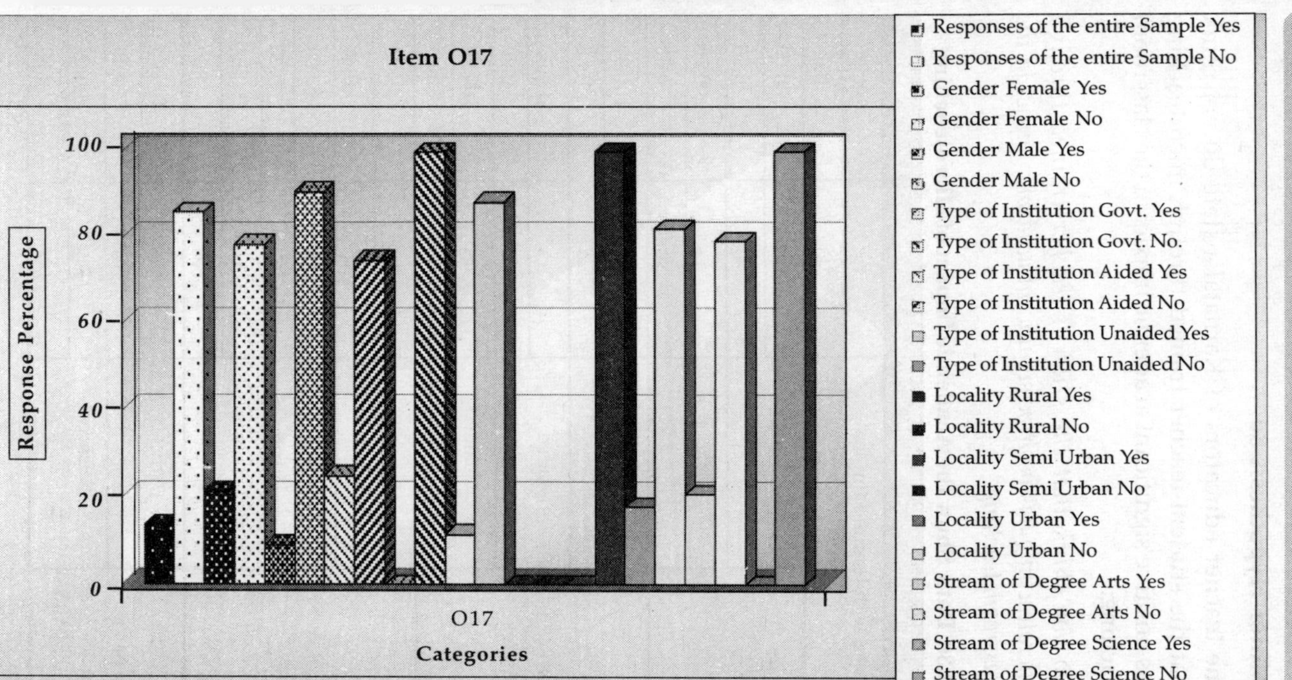

Graph 4.29: **Data Show Usage of Microteaching**

Null Minor Hypothesis 30

The teacher educators of Karnataka state do not think that the student-teacher trained through microteaching has positive significant academic impact in the classroom teaching.

O18: *Do you think that the student-teacher trained through microteaching has positive significant academic impact in the classroom teaching?*

Table 4.30: Data Show the Academic Impact of Microteaching

Variable		Responses	O18
Responses of the entire Sample		Yes	100.00
		No	0.00
Gender	Female	Yes	100.00
		No	0.00
	Male	Yes	100.00
		No	0.00
Type of Institution	Govt.	Yes	100.00
		No	0.00
	Aided	Yes	100.00
		No	0.00
	Unaided	Yes	100.00
		No	0.00
Locality	Rural	Yes	0.00
		No	0.00
	Semi-Urban	Yes	100.00
		No	0.00
	Urban	Yes	100.00
		No	0.00
Stream of Degree	Arts	Yes	100.00
		No	0.00
	Science	Yes	100.00
		No	0.00

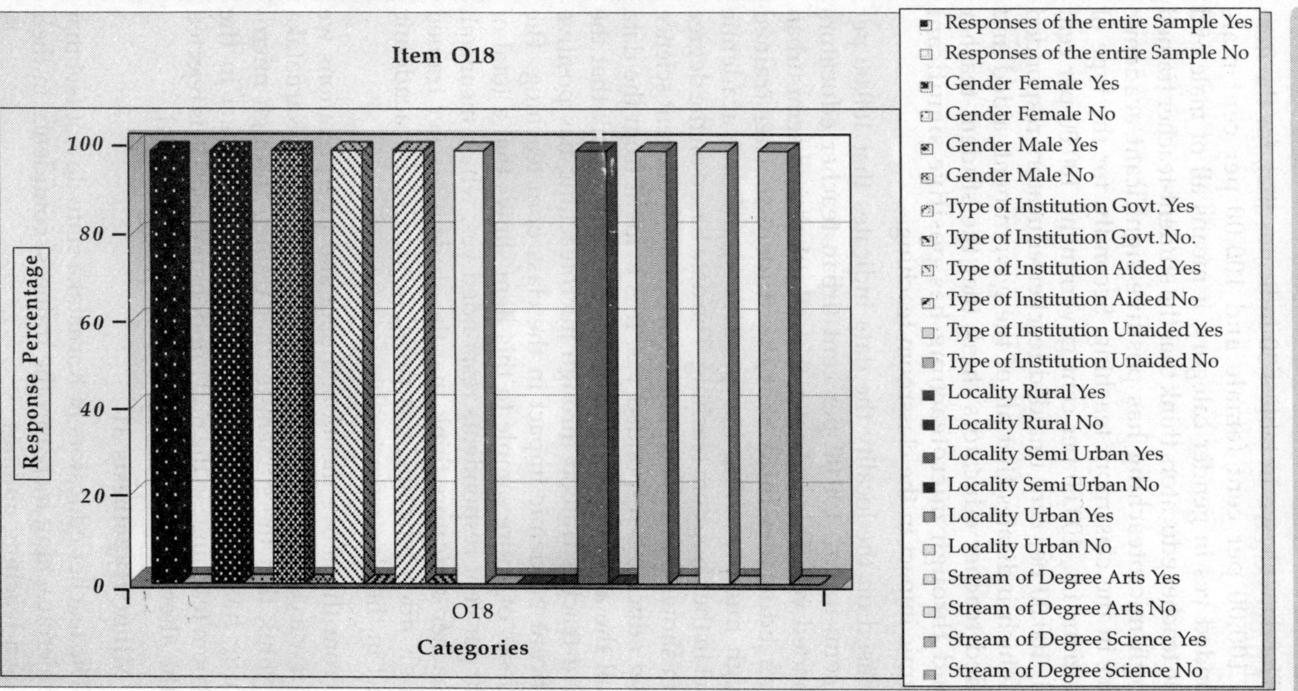

Graph 4.30: **Data Show the Academic Impact of Microteaching**

The data shown in table 4.30 indicates that, for the item O18, 100.00 per cent female and 100.00 per cent male responded yes in gender category, it means all of male and female teacher educators think that the student-teacher trained through microteaching has positive significant academic impact in the classroom teaching. Secondly, for the type of institutions i.e., 100.00 per cent government, 100.00 per cent aided, 100.00 per cent unaided teacher educators responded yes, which indicates that all of the government, aided and unaided teacher educators think that the student-teacher trained through microteaching has positive significant academic impact in the classroom teaching.

Based on the locality the data indicates that 100.00 per cent semi-urban, 100.00 per cent urban teacher educators responded yes. This indicates that all urban and semi-urban teacher educators think that the student-teacher trained through microteaching has positive significant academic impact in the classroom teaching. The data based on the degree stream shows that 100.00 per cent arts, 100.00 per cent science teacher educators responded yes. It is evident from the data that all the arts and science teacher educators think that the student-teacher trained through microteaching has positive significant academic impact in the classroom teaching. The responses of entire sample to this item shows that a total of 100.00 per cent respondents responded yes, which means all the teacher educators think that the student-teacher trained through microteaching has positive significant academic impact in the classroom teaching.

From the above mentioned data and interpretations we can draw a conclusion that the teacher educators of Karnataka state think that the student-teacher trained through micro-teaching has positive significant academic impact in the classroom teaching, so the null minor hypothesis 30 is rejected and the alternative minor hypothesis 30 is accepted.

Null Minor Hypothesis 31

The teacher educators of Karnataka state do not feel that microteaching increases the trainees' confidence in their own teaching abilities.

O19: *Do you feel that microteaching increases the trainees' confidence in their own teaching abilities?*

Table 4.31: Data Show Trainees' Confidence in Microteaching

Variable		Responses	O19
Responses of the entire Sample		Yes	100.00
		No	0.00
Gender	Female	Yes	100.00
		No	0.00
	Male	Yes	100.00
		No	0.00
Type of Institution	Govt.	Yes	100.00
		No	0.00
	Aided	Yes	100.00
		No	0.00
	Unaided	Yes	100.00
		No	0.00
Locality	Rural	Yes	0.00
		No	0.00
	Semi-Urban	Yes	100.00
		No	0.00
	Urban	Yes	100.00
		No	0.00
Stream of Degree	Arts	Yes	100.00
		No	0.00
	Science	Yes	100.00
		No	0.00

The data shown in table 4.31 indicates that, for the item O19, 100.00 per cent female and 100.00 per cent male responded yes in gender category, it means all of male and female teacher educators feel that microteaching increases the trainees' confidence in their own teaching abilities. Secondly, for the type of institutions i.e., 100.00 per cent government, 100.00 per cent aided, 100.00 per cent unaided teacher educators responded yes, which indicates that all of the government, aided and unaided teacher educators feel that

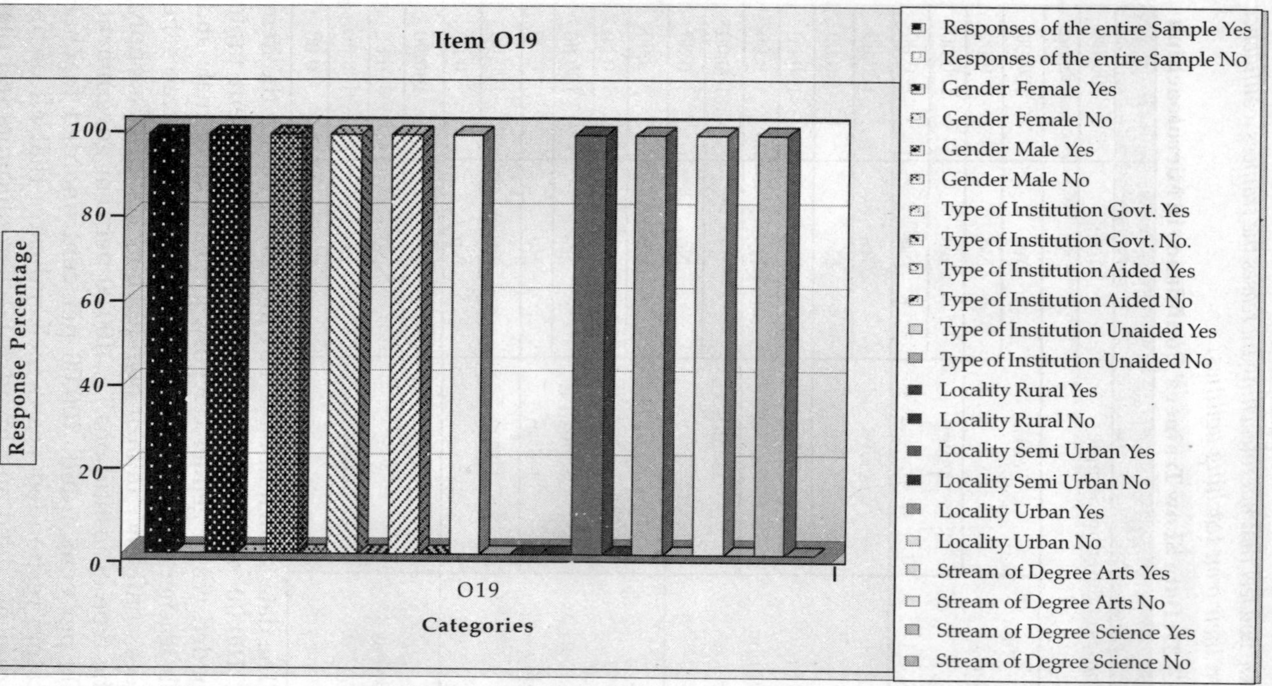

Graph 4.31: Data Show Trainees' Confidence in Microteaching

microteaching increases the trainees' confidence in their own teaching abilities. Based on the locality the data indicates that 100.00 per cent semi-urban, 100.00 per cent urban teacher educators responded yes. This indicates that all urban and semi-urban teacher educators feel that microteaching increases the trainees' confidence in their own teaching abilities.

The data based on the degree stream shows that 100.00 per cent arts, 100.00 per cent science teacher educators responded yes. It is evident from the data that all the arts and science teacher educators feel that microteaching increases the trainees' confidence in their own teaching abilities. The responses of entire sample to this item shows that a total of 100.00 per cent respondents responded yes, which means all the teacher educators feel that microteaching increases the trainees' confidence in their own teaching abilities.

From the above mentioned data and interpretations we can draw a conclusion that the teacher educators of Karnataka state feel that microteaching increases the trainees' confidence in their own teaching abilities, so the null minor hypothesis 31 is rejected and the alternative minor hypothesis 31 is accepted.

Null Minor Hypothesis 32

The teacher educators of Karnataka state do not agree that microteaching helps in preparing a good teacher.

O20: *Do you agree that microteaching helps in preparing a good teacher?*

The data shown in table 4.32 indicates that, for the item O20, 100.00 per cent female and 100.00 per cent male responded yes in gender category. It means all of male and female teacher educators agree that microteaching helps in preparing a good teacher.

Secondly, for the type of institutions i.e., 100.00 per cent government, 100.00 per cent aided, 100.00 per cent unaided teacher educators responded yes, which indicates that all of the government, aided and unaided teacher educators agree that microteaching helps in preparing a good teacher. Based

Table 4.32: Data Show Responses about Preparation of Good Teachers by Microteaching

Variable		Responses	O20
Responses of the entire Sample		Yes	100.00
		No	0.00
Gender	Female	Yes	100.00
		No	0.00
	Male	Yes	100.00
		No	0.00
Type of Institution	Govt.	Yes	100.00
		No	0.00
	Aided	Yes	100.00
		No	0.00
	Unaided	Yes	100.00
		No	0.00
Locality	Rural	Yes	0.00
		No	0.00
	Semi-Urban	Yes	100.00
		No	0.00
	Urban	Yes	100.00
		No	0.00
Stream of Degree	Arts	Yes	100.00
		No	0.00
	Science	Yes	100.00
		No	0.00

on the locality the data indicates that 100.00 per cent semi-urban, 100.00 per cent urban teacher educators responded yes. This indicates that all urban and semi-urban teacher educators agree that microteaching helps in preparing a good teacher. The data based on the degree stream shows that 100.00 per cent arts, 100.00 per cent science teacher educators responded yes. It is evident from the data that all the arts and science teacher educators agree that microteaching helps in preparing a good teacher. The responses of entire sample to this item shows that a total of 100.00 per cent respondents responded yes, which means all the teacher educators agree that microteaching helps in preparing a good teacher.

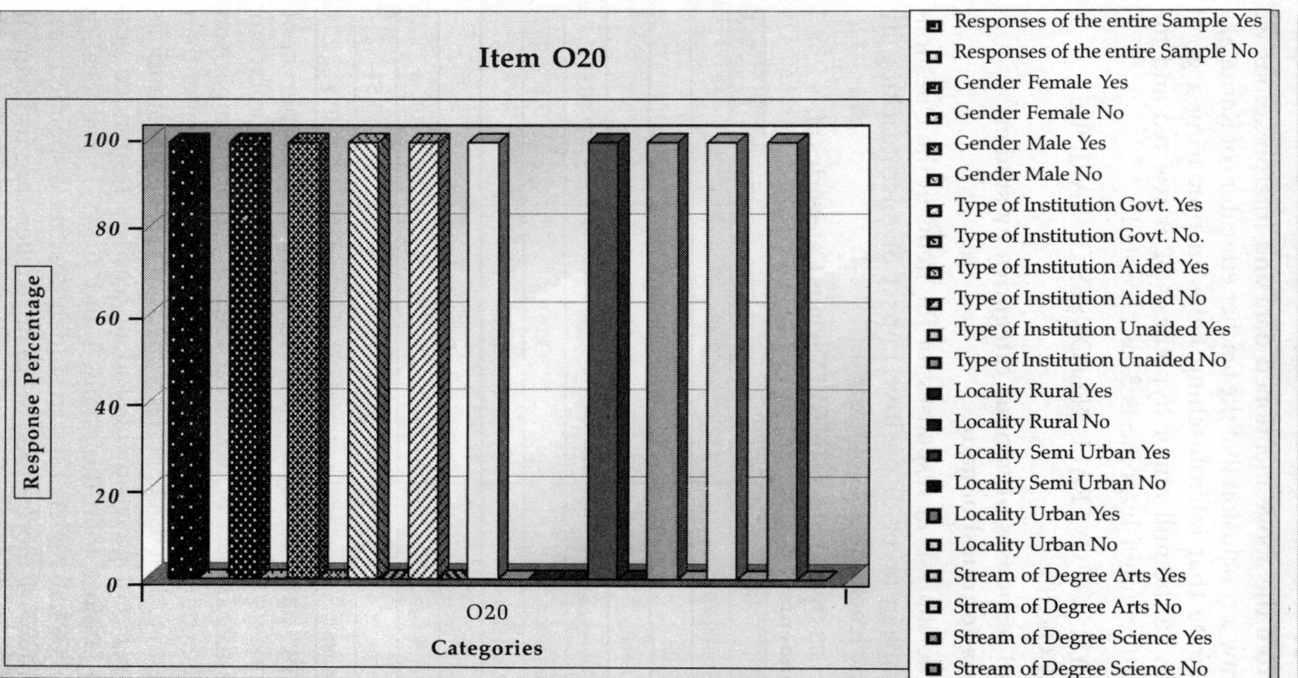

Graph 4.32: **Data Show Responses about Preparation of Good Teachers by Microteaching**

From the above mentioned data and interpretations we can draw a conclusion that the teacher educators of Karnataka state agree that microteaching helps in preparing a good teacher, so the null minor hypothesis 32 is rejected and the alternative minor hypothesis 32 is accepted.

ANALYSIS OF OVERALL RESPONSES OF VARIOUS CATEGORIES

Overall responses of various categories by student teachers for questionnaire.

The analysis of responses for the items in the Questionnaire are in favor of positive impact of microteaching by student teacher.

Table 4.33 Overall Responses of Various Categories of Respondents

Category	Yes (%)	No (%)
Total responses	92.80	7.19
Male	90.06	9.93
Female	94.68	5.31
Government	95.24	4.75
Unaided	92.16	7.83
Aided	92.12	7.87
Urban	94.89	5.10
Semi-Urban	81.70	18.29
Arts	94.45	5.54
Science	89.05	10.94

The data in table 4.33 show that 92.80 per cent respondents responded yes for the items which are in favour of positive impact of Microteaching. In gender comparison 94.68 per cent female responded yes and they are more than the male student teachers. Secondly, for the type of institutions 95.24 per cent government student teachers responded yes, which is more than the unaided and aided. In the locality category 94.89 per cent urban student teacher responded yes, which means more urban student teachers are in favor of positive impact of microteaching on them. Lastly 94.45 per cent student teachers from Arts background responded yes and this is more than the Science student teachers.

Overall responses of various categories by teacher educators for opinionnaire:

The analysis of responses for the items in the Opinionnaire is in favor of positive impact of microteaching by teacher educators.

Table 4.34: Overall Responses of various Categories by Teacher Educators

Category	Yes (%)	No (%)
Total responses	98.33	1.66
Male	97.27	2.77
Female	100.00	0.00
Government	99.16	0.83
Unaided	97.94	2.08
Aided	100.00	0.00
Urban	98.8	1.19
Semi-Urban	96.66	3.33
Arts	97.5	2.5
Science	100.00	0.00

Data from table 4.34 reveal that the overall responses in favours of microteaching are 98.33 per cent yes and 1.66 per cent no. This indicates that the teacher educators of Karnataka state find the positive impact of microteaching on the student teachers. While comparing the gender responses, it is found that 100 per cent female are in favour of microteaching and they are more than the male percentage of 97.27. In institutionwise comparison Aided institutions are 100 per cent in favour of positive impact of microteaching, which is more than the responses of government and unaided. As far as the locality is concerned 98.8 per cent urban and 96.66 per cent semi-urban teacher educators are in favour of microteaching's positive impact, which means that more number of urban teacher educators feel positive impact than the semi-urban. In Arts and Science categories, 100 per cent Science teacher educators are in favour of positive impact of microteaching than the Arts teacher educators who are 97.5 per cent in number.

Findings Showing Status of Microteaching

Overview

In this chapter the investigators sum up the whole research work, it starts from brief introduction and then restating the problems, the objectives prepared for the study, hypotheses formulated, the designing of sample, the instrumentation. The investigators also write the major findings of the study, limitations of the study and scope of the further research.

Introduction

Teaching is a highly skilled job and therefore requires adequate training. Every teacher must have a clear understanding of his task, its meaning and intricacies involved. It is a system of actions intended to induce learning. The goals of education cannot be achieved unless teachers have the necessary skills and competencies. The skills and competencies can be developed through systematic approach to revitalise and modernise teacher education.

Earlier it was accepted that "teachers are born not made" but now a slogan has come that "a teacher is made but not born".

Now in education technology many techniques have come which can be used to train the teacher for effective teaching, one among these techniques is microteaching.

Microteaching is a scaled-down, simulated teaching encounter designed for the training of both pre-service and in-service teachers. Its purpose is to provide teachers with the opportunity for the safe practice of an enlarged cluster of teaching skills while learning how to develop simple, single-concept lessons in any teaching subject. Microteaching helps teachers improve both content and methods of teaching and develop specific teaching skills such as questioning, the use of examples and simple artefacts to make lessons more interesting, effective reinforcement techniques, and introducing and closing lessons effectively. Immediate, focused feedback and encouragement, combined with the opportunity to practice the suggested improvements in the same training session, are the foundations of microteaching protocols.

Microteaching is a training technique which requires student teachers to teach a single concept using specified teaching skill to a small number of pupils in a short duration of time. The most important point in microteaching is that teaching is practised in terms of definable, observable, measurable and controllable teaching skills.

1. Allen, D.W. (1966): Microteaching is a scaled down teaching encounter in class size and class time.
2. Allen, D.W. and Eve, A. W. (1968): Microteaching is defined as a system of controlled practice that makes it possible to concentrate on specified teaching behaviour and to practice teaching under controlled conditions.
3. Munn (1966): Microteaching as a "scaled down teaching encounter in class size and class time".
4. Buch, R.N. (1968): Microteaching is a trainer education technique which allows the teacher to apply well-defined teaching skills to a carefully prepared lesson in a planned series of five to ten minutes, encounter with a small group of real classroom students often with an opportunity to observe the performance on video-tape.

Microteaching was developed only a decade ago, but in comparison with many other innovations in education, it has been adopted very quickly by many teacher educators in developed countries. However, its adoption in developing countries has been somewhat slower, mainly as a result of the notion that the use of laboratory systems, and in particular microteaching, is inherently dependent on the use of hardware and specially video-tape recorders. Such equipment is very difficult to obtain in some developing countries both because of its relatively high cost and because of technical difficulties of operation and maintenance.

Teaching constitute of many stages and skills, methods, tactics, techniques etc. If teaching skills are integrated and used in classroom then teaching becomes effective. So the student teacher should be trained to teach in classroom with different skills. All the skills together cannot be taught at once, so skills are presented one after another. The technique which gives the better way of teaching is "Microteaching". Before going to the classroom if microteaching training is provided to the student teachers definitely they perform very well in practice teaching. In this study the investigators have tried to know the effectiveness of microteaching and its impact on the student teachers and also tried to know how much the student teachers of Karnataka state know about microteaching and whether they are practicing it. Now, the microteaching has become the part of the course of college of teacher education. Therefore, the investigators have studied different related research studies to get the direction for the present study. After studying all the researches the investigators get idea to study about how much the student teachers know about microteaching. How they use it and what is its impact on their teaching.

Problem Restated

The statement of the problem is,

"To study the impact of microteaching on student-teachers of colleges of education in Karnataka".

Microteaching is gradually becoming the important part of teacher training institute, so in this study the investigators wanted to know it, using it and what affect the microteaching is putting on the student teachers, particularly in Karnataka State's Secondary Level Teacher Training institutes.

Objectives

- To study the impact of microteaching on student teacher.
- To study the use of microteaching in different Solleges of Education in Karnataka state.
- To study the perception of microteaching by teacher educators.

HYPOTHESES

Null Major Hypothesis

"There is no positive impact of microteaching on the student teachers of College of Education in Karnataka state."

Null Minor Hypotheses

1. The student teachers of Karnataka state are not well versed with the meaning of microteaching.
2. The student teachers of Karnataka state do not know the objectives of microteaching.
3. The student teachers of Karnataka state do not know the main purpose of microteaching.
4. The student teachers of Karnataka state cannot explain the different components of microteaching.
5. The student teachers of Karnataka state do not practice the microteaching skills.
6. The student teachers of Karnataka state do not practice the microteaching cycle.
7. The student teachers of Karnataka state do not know the method of microteaching lesson plan.
8. The student teachers of Karnataka state do not involve in organisation of microteaching.

9. The student teachers of Karnataka state do not observe the microteaching lesson plans by using observation schedule.
10. The student teachers of Karnataka state do not know the planning of microteaching.
11. The student teachers of Karnataka state do not know the importance of feedback.
12. The student teachers of Karnataka state do not get the demonstration of microteaching skills.
13. The teacher educators of Karnataka state do not think that microteaching cycle should be introduced compulsorily to the student-teachers of B.Ed. course.
14. The teacher educators of Karnataka state do not feel it is necessary for teacher educators of B.Ed. to demonstrate all the skills of microteaching.
15. The teacher educators of Karnataka state face difficulty in demonstrating microteaching skills.
16. The teacher educators of Karnataka state feel that training through microteaching is laborious for both student-teachers and their supervisors.
17. The teacher educators of Karnataka state feel that training through microteaching is time consuming technique.
18. The teacher educators of Karnataka state do not feel that training through microteaching improves the practicing skills of student-teachers.
19. The teacher educators of Karnataka state do not feel that microteaching helps in improving teaching competency.
20. The teacher educators of Karnataka state do not think that observation play an important role in microteaching.
21. The teacher educators of Karnataka state do not think that feedback helps in improving the skills.
22. The teacher educators of Karnataka state do not think that audio-vide recording tools are good for feedback.

23. The teacher educators of Karnataka state do not think that microteaching gradually teaches integration of various teaching skills.
24. The teacher educators of Karnataka state feel that student-teachers feel boredom during practice of teaching skills.
25. The teacher educators of Karnataka state do not agree that their student teachers practice microteaching skills in accordance with microteaching cycle.
26. The teacher educators of Karnataka state do not agree that their student teacher perform the microteaching enthusiastically.
27. The teacher educators of Karnataka state do not teach minimum of 6 microteaching skills to their students.
28. The teacher educators of Karnataka state do not agree that student teachers practice at least 6 microteaching skills.
29. The teacher educators of Karnataka state think that student teachers want to go for practice teaching directly without undergoing microteaching.
30. The teacher educators of Karnataka state do not think that the student-teacher trained through microteaching has positive significant academic impact in the classroom teaching.
31. The teacher educators of Karnataka state do not feel that microteaching increases the trainees' confidence in their own teaching abilities.
32. The teacher educators of Karnataka state do not agree that microteaching helps in preparing a good teacher.

Alternative Major Hypothesis

"There is a positive impact of microteaching on the student teachers of College of Education in Karnataka state."

Alternative Minor Hypotheses

1. The student teachers of Karnataka state are well versed with the meaning of microteaching.
2. The student teachers of Karnataka state know the objectives of microteaching.
3. The student teachers of Karnataka state know the main purpose of microteaching.
4. The student teachers of Karnataka State can explain the different components of microteaching.
5. The student teachers of Karnataka state practice the microteaching skills.
6. The student teachers of Karnataka state practice the microteaching cycle.
7. The student teachers of Karnataka state know the method of microteaching lesson plan.
8. The student teachers of Karnataka state involved in organisation of microteaching.
9. The student teachers of Karnataka state observe the microteaching lesson plans by using observation schedule.
10. The student teachers of Karnataka state know the planning of microteaching.
11. The student teachers of Karnataka state know the importance of feedback.
12. The student teachers of Karnataka state get the demonstration of microteaching skills.
13. The student teachers of Karnataka state think that microteaching cycle should be introduced compulsorily to the student-teachers of B.Ed. course.
14. The student teachers of Karnataka state feel it is necessary for teacher educators of B.Ed. to demonstrate all the skills of microteaching.

15. The student teachers of Karnataka state do not face difficulty in demonstrating microteaching skills.
16. The teacher educators of Karnataka state do not feel that training through microteaching is laborious for both student-teachers and their supervisors.
17. The teacher educators of Karnataka state do not feel that training through microteaching is time consuming technique.
18. The teacher educators of Karnataka state feel that training through microteaching improves the practicing skills of student-teachers.
19. The teacher educators of Karnataka state feel that microteaching helps in improving teaching competency.
20. The teacher educators of Karnataka state think that observation play an important role in microteaching.
21. The teacher educators of Karnataka state think that feedback helps in improving the skills.
22. The teacher educators of Karnataka state think that audio-vide recording tools are good for feedback.
23. The teacher educators of Karnataka state think that microteaching gradually teaches integration of various teaching skills.
24. The teacher educators of Karnataka state do not feel that student-teachers feel boredom during practice of teaching skills.
25. The teacher educators of Karnataka state agree that their student teachers practice microteaching skills in accordance with microteaching cycle.
26. The teacher educators of Karnataka state agree that their student teacher perform the microteaching enthusiastically.
27. The teacher educators of Karnataka state teach minimum of 6 microteaching skills to their students.

28. The teacher educators of Karnataka state agree that student teachers practice at least 6 microteaching skills.
29. The teacher educators of Karnataka state do not think that student teachers want to go for practice teaching directly without undergoing microteaching.
30. The teacher educators of Karnataka state think that the student-teacher trained through microteaching has positive significant academic impact in the classroom teaching.
31. The teacher educators of Karnataka state feel that microteaching increases the trainees' confidence in their own teaching abilities.
32. The teacher educators of Karnataka state agree that microteaching helps in preparing a good teacher.

Sampling Design

A sample is a small population selected for observation and analysis. By observing the characteristics of the sample, one can make certain inferences about the characteristics of the population from which it is drawn.

Sampling technique used: In Karnataka state there are 360 colleges of Education for Secondary School Teacher Training. There are four revenue divisions in Karnataka state, the investigators attempted for representative samples from each division. The investigators used purposive random sampling method and among these 4 divisions the investigators have chosen 22 colleges of Education randomly. The following Table 5.1 indicates the number of College of Education taken for sampling.

Table 5.1: Number of Sample Colleges

S. No.	Division	No. of Colleges
1	Belgaum	13
2	Gulbarga	5
3	Bangalore	3
4	Mysore	1

The total sample taken for the study contains 220 student teachers and 44 teacher educators from different secondary level teacher training institutes of Karnataka state.

Tools

The investigators have prepared the tool that is questionnaire for student teachers and opinionnaire for teacher educators. First the investigators prepared 60 items for questionnaire and 24 items for opinionnaire then gave it to the guide. After editing by the guide the tools were given to expert educationist like Deans and Professors of education and other research expert. The corrections suggested by the concerned were incorporated and tools were administered on a small sample of student teachers and teacher educators from the host institution i.e. Maulana Azad National Urdu University, Hyderabad where the investigators are working for standardisation of the tool. A sample of 50 student teachers and 10 teacher educators was used. The difficult item, double drum items or items with content errors were removed and simple items were replaced in consultation with the guide. The final questionnaire consisted of 36 items and was administered on the student teachers. The opinionnaire consisted of 20 items and it was administered on the teacher educators.

The questionnaire is made up of 36 different items which are divided in 12 sections which are grouped in 12 sections of 3 items each.

Procedure of Data Collection

The investigators sent 10 questionnaire and 2 opinionnaires to each of the College of Education taken as sample by post. These questionnaires and opinionnaires were accompanied by the introduction letter of the guide and request letter of the investigators with detailed instructions. Further, a self-addressed stamped envelop was also placed for ensuring feedback from the concerned college. The investigators also followed the post through phone. The sampled institutions were asked to send the filled-in tools in the self-addressed stamped envelop sent by the investigators. Some of the institutes sent immediate feedback and some delayed it. A reminder and letter of gratitude was also sent to the concerned institutes. Further, interaction was made through phone to ensure more responses. This has helped the investigators to obtain feedback from most of the institutes. However, few of the institutes apologise for not responding as the vacation had commenced for the student teachers and they were not available. The investigators have conveyed gratitude to all the institutes for their concern towards research in the field of education.

Findings

The major findings of the present study are:

1. The student teachers of Karnataka state are well versed with the meaning, purpose, objectives component of microteaching.
2. The student teachers of Karnataka state prepare the micro-lesson plan and practice microteaching skills according to microteaching cycle.
3. The student teachers do the observation of microteaching lessons and also give the proper feedback through feed-back technique.
4. The teacher educators give sufficient demonstration for microteaching skills.
5. Teacher educators feel it is necessary for teacher educators of B.Ed to demonstrate all the skills of micro teaching.
6. Teacher educators do not feel that training through microteaching is laborious for both student-teachers and their supervisors.
7. Teacher educators do not feel that training through microteaching is time consuming technique.
8. Teacher educators feel that training through micro-teaching improves the practicing skills of student teachers.

9. Teacher educators feel microteaching helps in improving teaching competency.
10. Teacher educators think that observation plays an important role in microteaching.
11. Teacher educators think that feedback helps in improving the skills.
12. Teacher educators think that audio-video recording tools are good for feedback.
13. Teacher educators think that microteaching gradually teaches integration of various teaching skills.
14. Teacher educators do not feel that student-teachers feel boredom during practice of teaching skills.
15. Student-teachers practice microteaching skills in accordance with microteaching cycle.
16. Student-teacher perform the microteaching enthusiastically.
17. Teacher educators teach minimum of 6 microteaching skills to your students.
18. Student-teachers perform at least 6 microteaching skill.
19. Teacher educators do not think that student-teachers want to go for practice teaching directly without undergoing microteaching.
20. Teacher educators think that the student-teacher trained through microteaching has positive significant academic impact in the classroom teaching.
21. Teacher educators feel that microteaching increases the trainees' confidence in their own teaching abilities.
22. Teacher educators agree that microteaching helps in preparing a good teacher.
23. In most of the College of Education microteaching is made compulsory for the student teachers.
24. There is a positive impact of microteaching on the student teachers of Karnataka state.

25. The female student teachers are more in favour of positive impact of microteaching as compared to male.
26. Student teachers studying in government institution are more in favour of positive impact of microteaching than the aided and unaided.
27. The urban area student teachers favour for having positive impact of microteaching than the semi-urban student teachers.
28. Arts student teachers are more in favour of microteaching than the science student teachers.
29. The female teacher educators are more in favour of positive impact of microteaching than the male teacher educators.
30. Aided institution teacher educators are more in favour of positive impact of microteaching than their aided and unaided counterparts.
31. The teacher educators belonging to urban area are more in favour of positive impact of microteaching.
32. Science teacher educators are more in favour of positive impact of microteaching than the Arts teacher educators.

The investigators have found a sound impact of use of microteaching in the teacher education institutes.

Use of microteaching has made the student teachers aware of the meaning, purpose, objectives component of microteaching. They prepare their micro-lesson plan, practice microteaching skills, which are most essential and positive habits before entering in the classroom. This has helped them in the observation of others lessons, giving of feedback and in turn acceptance of similar response from others, which help in learning of teaching. This methodology of teaching has increased interaction among teacher educators and student teachers, initially the former demonstrates lessons and the latter observers, whereas the reverse cycle takes place in the later half in which teacher educators also gives the feedback.

This small cohesive interactive group helps in development of perfect skills. There is negligible number of respondents who agree that microteaching is time consuming, waste of time, laborious or boring, which means that all most all the respondent agree with the importance of training before going to the actual classroom. It encourages the person to take up teaching, enhances power of observation, power of toleration and learn from the observations of others. It enhances use of audio-video material. The teaching is not only broken into different skills and its components but, the student-teachers learn to integrate various components, skills and practices it, which is essential for a general classroom.

Teacher educators feel that microteaching improves teaching competency, student-teachers learn by observation, oral and audio-visual feedback of peers and supervisors. Teacher-educators find their student motivated, learning skills together and appreciating feedback. This has made students practice teaching, before actually going to practice, i.e. at least 6 skills are practiced before entering the classroom. This mode of training has increased confidence level in student-teachers, which in turn has positive impact on student in the classrooms. This has helped in preparation of teachers who have positive impact on learners.

Hence, from above findings and discussions, it can be concluded that there is a positive impact of microteaching on the student teachers of secondary level teacher training institute of Karnataka state.

Limitations of the Study

1. This study is limited only to the Karnataka state.
2. This study is limited only to the secondary level teacher training institutes.

Scope of the further research

1. For further research it can be studied about how microteaching is helping the student teachers for effective teaching.

2. To study about which type of microteaching helps in practicing more skills.
3. To prepare the best macro-lesson by using microteaching lesson plans.
4. To study how many micro-teaching skills are required for preparing a best macro-lesson.
5. A comparison of the teaching competency of the student teachers trained by micro-teaching and traditional method.

Bibliography

1. http://eccarta.msn.com/dictionary_1861629873 micro-teaching.html
2. http://fdc.fullerton.edu/learning/CASTL/carnegic microteaching-materials.htm.
3. http://isitrs.harvard.edu/fs/html/microteaching.html
4. http://www.gradschool.uky.edu/MICROTEACHING pdf.
5. http://www.informaworld.com/smpp/content control + a 743954633.
6. Aggarwal, J.C., Essentials of Educational Technology: Teaching Learning, New Delhi, Vikas Publishing House, 2004.
7. Ahuja, Ram, Research Method, Jaipur, Rawat Publication, 2003.
8. Ameena Ebraheem Al-Methan (2003), "Merits of Microteaching as Perceived by Student Teachers at Kuwait University", *Journal Pendidikan* 28, pp.65-76.
9. Anne How, "Transfer of Educational Technology", *International Year Book of Educational & Instructional Technology, 1980-81.*

10. Arye Perlberg, "Recent approaches on microteaching and Allied techniques which can be implemented basically in developing countries", 1975.

11. Bhatia, S.K., (1984), "Microteaching With & Without Integration Training using Additive Dimension with Peer Supervisor Feedback under Simulated & Real Conditions", PhD Edu, JMI.

12. Bhatt, B.D., *Modern Indian Education Planning And Developemnt*, New Delhi, Kanishaka Publishers, 2006.

13. Bhattacharjee R., (1981), *Effectiveness of Microteaching in Developing Teaching Competence*, Extension Service Department, Post-Graduate Training College, Shillong.

14. Bhattacharya Dipak Kumar, *Research Methodology*, New Delhi, Excel Book, 2006.

15 Bhattachraya, D.K., *Research Methodology*, New Delhi, Excel Books, 2004.

16 Bryman Alan, *Social Research Methods*, New York, Oxford University Press, 2001.

17. Chakraborti Mohit, *Teacher Education Modern Trends*, New Delhi, Kanishka Publishers, 2006.

18. Chauhan, S.S., *Innovations in Teaching Learning Process*, Delhi, Vikas Publishing House Pvt Ltd., 2003.

19. Clift, J.C., and other (1980), "A Cost Effectiveness Study of the Use of Microteaching in the Education of Teachers", *British Journal of Educational Technology*, Vol. II, Issues 2.

20. Compiled by University Teaching Services, "Guide of Microteaching for the Instructional Skills Programme", 2006.

21. Dasgupta, D.N., *Practice Teaching*, Jaipur, Pointer Publishers, 2002.

22. Dash, Biranchi Narayan, *Teacher And Education in the Emerging Indian Society* Vol. II, Hyderabad, Neelkamal Publications, 2007.

23. Dave, C.S., "Relative effectiveness of microteaching having the summative model of integration versus the mini-teaching model in terms of general teaching competence, teacher attitude towards teaching, pupil-liking & pupil achievement", PhD Edu, Devi Ahilya.

24. Dutta, Ram (1990), "Integration in microteaching", *Indian Educational Review*, Vol. 25 (1).

25. Dwivedi, Jagdishwar (1988), "An investigation into the Effectiveness of Microteaching in the Development of Psychomotor Skills in Biology Practicals", PhD, Edu, University of Allahbad.

26. Gandhi, K.A. (1992), "Microteaching Approach for Student-Teachers", *The Progress of Education,* Vol. 67(1).

27. Ghanta, Ramesh, Dash, B.N, *Foundations of Education*, Hyderabad, Neelkamal Publication, Hyderabad, 2006.

28. Ghose, B.N., *Scientific Methods and Social Research*, Sterling, New Delhi, 1982.

29. Gor, Kantilal Visanji (1992), " A Study of the Effectiveness of Microteaching Strategies for Developming the Teaching Competency of Primary Teacher-Trainees", PhD., Edu, Saurashtra Uni, Fifth survey of educational Research.

30. Harry, Mayhew, C., *Developing Teaching Skills with Microteaching*, Morehead State University, 1982.

31. Joshi Sunita, Sharma Abha, *Micro Teaching a Practical Approach*, Delhi, Authors Press, 2006.

32. Julice Gess & others, *The Preservice Microteaching Course & Science Teachers' Instructional Decisions: A Qualitative Analysis*, Department of Science & Mathematics Education", Oregon State Uni, Corvallis, Oregon.

33. Kalyanpurkar, S., (1986), "The Effect of Microteaching on the Teaching Competence of Inservice Teachers & its Impact on Pupil's Attainment & Pupil's Liking", PhD Edu, DAVV.

34. Kothari,C.R., *Research Methodology Methods and Techniques*, New Delhi, New Age International Publisher, 2007.

35. Koul Lokesh, *Methodology of Educational Research*, Vikas Publisher, New Delhi, 1997.

36. Kumar, K.L., *Educational Technology*, New Delhi, New Age International Publishers, 2001.

37. Lal Das, D.K., *Design of Social Research*, Rawat Publication, Jaipur, 2005.

38. Mayhew, Harry C., *Developing Teaching Skills with Microteaching*, 1982.

39. Mohantay, Jagannath, *Modern Trends in Educational Technologgy*, Hyderabad, Neelkamal, 2005.

40. Mohd. Sharif Khan, *Educational Research*, New Delhi, Ashish Publishing House, 1990.

41. Mygeri, C.V., *Educational Technology*, Gadag, Vidyanidhi Prakashana, 2005.

42. Naik, V.V (1984), "A comparative study of the Effect of Microteaching & Conventional Approaches of Teacher Training upon Pupils' Achievement, Pupils' Perception & General Teaching Competence of Pre-service Student Teachers", PhD Edu, Bombay University.

43. Nancy D.Bell (2007), "Microteaching: What is it That is Going on here?", Department of English, Indiana University of Pennsylvania, Leonard Hall, Indiana, US.

44. Palekar S.A., *Research Methods in Social Science*, Current Publications, Agra, 2007.

45. Panneerselvam, R., *Research Methodology*, New Delhi, Prentice Hall of India, 2006.

46. Ram Babu, Dandapani, S., *Essentials of Microteaching*, Hyderabad, Neelkamal Publication, 2007.

47 Rather, A. R., *Essentials of Instructional Technology*, New Delhi, Discovery Publishing House, 2004.

48. Sharma, Shashi Prabha, *Basic Principles of Education*, New Delhi, Kanishka Publishers.

59. Sharma, B.A.V (ed.) *Research Methods in Social Science*, New Sterling Publishers, New Delhi, 1983.

50. Siddiqui Mujabul Hasan, *Technology in Teacher Education*, APH Publishing Corporation, 2004.

51. Singh, L.C., Sharma, R.D, *Microteaching Theory and Practice*, Agra, H.P. Bhargava Book House.

52. Tandon, B.C., *Research Methodology in Social Sciences*, Chitanya Publishing House, Allahabad, 1979.

53. Tara Chand, *Educational Technology*, New Delhi, Anmol Publications, 2002.

54. Vanaja, M., Rajasekar, S., *Educational Technology and Computer Education*, Hyderabad, Neelkamal Publications, 2006.

55. Wilkinson, T. S. and Bhandarkar, P.L., *Methodology and Techniques of Social Research*, Bombay: Himalaya, 1977.

56. Young Pauline V, *Scientific Social Surveys and Research*, Printice Hall, New Delhi, 1992.

Index

❑❑❑